COUNSELLING IN
CAREERS GUIDANCE

· COUNSELLING IN CONTEXT ·

Series editors
Moira Walker and Michael Jacobs

Counselling takes place in many different contexts: in voluntary and statutory agencies; in individual private practice or in a consortium; at work, in medical settings, in churches and in different areas of education. While there may be much in common in basic counselling methods (despite theoretical differences), each setting gives rise to particular areas of concern, and often requires specialist knowledge, both of the problems likely to be brought, but also of the context in which the client is being seen. Even common counselling issues vary slightly from situation to situation in the way they are applied and understood.

This series examines twelve such areas, and applies a similar scheme to each, first looking at the history of the development of counselling in that particular context; then at the context itself, and how the counsellor fits into it. Central to each volume are chapters on common issues related to the specific setting and questions that may be peculiar to it but could be of interest and value to counsellors working elsewhere. Each book will provide useful information for anyone considering counselling, or the provision of counselling in a particular context. Relationships with others who work in the same setting whether as counsellors, managers or administrators are also examined; and each book concludes with the author's own critique of counselling as it is currently practised in that context.

Current and forthcoming titles

Elsa Bell: *Counselling in Further and Higher Education*
Judith Brearley: *Counselling and Social Work*
Dilys Davies: *Counselling in Psychological Services*
Patricia East: *Counselling in Medical Settings*
Annette Greenwood: *Workplace Counselling*
Migel Jayasinghe: *Counselling in Careers Guidance*
David Lyall: *Counselling in the Pastoral and Spiritual Context*
Judith Mabey and Bernice Sorensen: *Counselling for Young People*
Janet Perry: *Counselling for Women*
Gabrielle Syme: *Counselling in Independent Practice*
Nicholas Tyndall: *Counselling in the Voluntary Sector*
Brian Williams: *Counselling in Criminal Justice*

COUNSELLING IN CAREERS GUIDANCE

Migel Jayasinghe

OPEN UNIVERSITY PRESS
Buckingham · Philadelphia

Open University Press
Celtic Court
22 Ballmoor
Buckingham
MK18 1XW

email: enquiries@openup.co.uk
world wide web: www.openup.co.uk

and
325 Chestnut Street
Philadelphia, PA 19106, USA

First Published 2001

A catalogue record of this book is available from the British Library

ISBN   0 335 20396 5 (pb)

Library of Congress Cataloging-in-Publication Data
Jayasinghe, Migel, 1936-
Counselling in careers guidance / Migel Jayasinghe.
p.   cm. - (Counselling in context)
Includes bibliographical references and index.
ISBN 0- 335- 20396- 5
1. Vocational guidance- United States- History.   2. Vocational guidance-
Great Britain- History.   I. Title.   II. Series.
HF5382.5.U5 J39   2001
158.6- dc21   00- 034709

Typeset by Graphicraft Limited, Hong Kong
Printed in Great Britain by St Edmundsbury Press, Bury St Edmunds

This book is dedicated to the memory of my 'vernacular' schoolteacher father who died on 15 October 1999 in Sri Lanka aged 92. He was a great storyteller.

Contents

Series editors' preface

Freud described the principal goals of life as 'to love and to work'. Psychotherapy and counselling have devoted much thought and focus to the need to love and to be loved, concentrating almost exclusively on relationships between people, and within themselves. Work has received in comparison very much less attention, although it clearly occupies a significant proportion of each person's life, is for most people their sole means of surviving financially, and of course in itself involves relationships which often mirror those of the family.

Work-place counselling, employee assistance programmes in particular, have over recent years helped to correct the imbalance in counselling's concentration upon the personal and domestic arenas. This context for counselling is the subject of another title in this series. But there is another area of the world of work, which has its own significance, seen in the terms often used to describe it such as 'career' or 'vocation'. Here is a concept which over-arches dynamics of the day-to-day working environment. The notion of career or vocation ties up very closely with who a person is, where their personal strengths and skills lie, what their temperament disposes them towards, what they are seeking from work in addition to a salary or wage. It is that which is the subject of this book, and the object of this particular counselling in context.

Counselling has in fact always been closely connected with guidance: 'marriage guidance' preceded relationship counselling; careers advice and guidance was one of the foundations upon which counselling was built, perhaps more in the United States than in Britain and Europe, but nonetheless reflected in the title of the *British Journal of Advice and Counselling*; the precise position of counselling between advice and guidance on the one hand and psychotherapy on the other was one of the issues in the development of National Vocational Qualifications, and we note the term vocational again here. But just as marriage guidance has changed, so has careers guidance, and Migel Jayasinghe's book makes this very clear, illustrating the present context with examples from the United States and Europe, as well as pointing up the comparative dearth of resources in the careers field in Britain.

He observes that the concept of vocation, at least in terms of a life-long personal identification with a particular form of work, has changed. The notion of 'career' must be understood far more widely than we have been accustomed to, and for much longer than the former concern with helping young people find the right kind of job. We may live currently in a society where the worst excesses of unemployment, so familiar in the eighties, have been overcome, but we still live in an economic and social climate where changes of job, fluidity of employment, and indeed the objectives of earning a living have considerably altered.

Those whose work is principally concerned with enabling others to train for and find work will find in this book much to reflect upon that may encourage them to use the skills which counselling has developed and perhaps might give back to one of its 'parent' bodies. But this is a book also for generic counsellors, who inevitably engage with clients for whom issues of work and at work are a feature of their lives. 'Work' may appear to be limited to eight-to-six, nine-to-five or flexi-time, but it spills over into the rest of life, just as the rest of life often spills over into it (something which companies have recognized in their desire to use EAP's). But more than that: a client will often be searching not only for 'who I am', but also for 'what I want to do or achieve', whether 'in my job' or 'with my life' or 'next' or 'before I retire'. Counsellors will indeed often have had to consider these questions for themselves, as they have themselves often changed direction from one sort of work to another. This book provides much for counsellors and therapists in general to reflect upon in relation to society, their clients, and themselves.

Moira Walker
Michael Jacobs

Acknowledgements

Thanks are due to many individuals who helped to make this book a reality. I gained invaluable field experience in setting up the Royal British Legion Industries' Vocational Assessment Centre, the brainchild of Mrs Patricia Wheeler, the current Welfare Manager. Professional colleagues who extended help and advice include Professor Audrey Collin of De Montfort University, Jeanie Stevens of Kent Adult Careers Guidance, and Hazel Reid and Alison Fielding of the College of Guidance Studies. Support from Jacinta Evans, from the publishers, was always forthcoming. Finally, I owe the deepest debt of gratitude to my critic, coach and guide, the series editor, Michael Jacobs, whose relentless pursuit of relevance and immediacy saved me from going off at a tangent all too often. I am however, fully responsible for errors and omissions, and would be grateful for any constructive feedback from my discerning readers.

· ONE ·

The development of counselling in careers guidance

The beginnings and development of vocational guidance can be traced to many diverse practices, theories, personalities, movements, and state interventions, which are steeped in controversy to this day. Before the Industrial Revolution changed patterns of employment forever, work as a means of earning a livelihood in agrarian societies was hereditary, hierarchical, and more or less fixed for a lifetime and even for generations. During these times there was hardly any change from inherited caste, class or occupation from father to son, in a society where the male was seen as the main breadwinner. This state of affairs was the lot of the majority, and the rightness of 'the rich man in his castle and the poor man at his gate' went unquestioned. Landowners had what were called 'private incomes' and the mass of people, the peasants, lived on the land, later becoming the industrial working class. In Europe between the sixteenth and eighteenth centuries 'daily life unfolded within the frame of enduring gender and social hierarchies' (Csikszenmihalyi 1997: 6).

When it came to child labour there was no sex discrimination.

A boy of six or seven years, born into a poor family in one of the industrial regions of England two hundred years ago, was likely to wake up around five in the morning, rush to the mill to service the clanking mechanical looms till sunset, six days a week. Often he would die of exhaustion before reaching his teens. A girl of twelve in the silk-making regions of France around the same time would sit next to a tub all day, dipping silkworm cocoons in scalding water to melt the sticky substance that held the threads together. She was likely to succumb to respiratory diseases as she sat in wet clothes from dawn to dusk, and her fingertips lost all feeling from the hot water. In the meantime, the children of the nobility learned to dance the minuet and to converse in foreign languages.

(Csikszenmihalyi 1997: 6)

The world has changed almost unrecognizably since then. The Protestant work ethic, the rise of the middle class, trades unions, mass movements, political revolutions, the bureaucracy, the end of the slave trade, the limited liability company, colonialism, science and technology, new inventions, mass communication, the division and mobility of labour, the growth of factories ('dark satanic mills'), urbanization, secularization, the spread of democracy, socialism, and world trade, are only a few of the antecedents which historians identify as forces that made inevitable the need for diverse and novel occupations and careers at the beginning of the twentieth century. While the process of change continues relentlessly, the need for guidance, and increasingly for counselling, in the choice, preparation, skill acquisition, maintenance, change and cessation of work, vocation or occupation, becomes ever more imperative for the vast majority of people.

ORIGINS OF VOCATIONAL GUIDANCE

Psychology, and later a specialism known as vocational psychology in the USA, or as industrial (later occupational) psychology in Britain, provided a 'scientific' approach to career guidance early in the twentieth century. Although psychology as a science reportedly developed in Germany at the end of the nineteenth century, its application to practical affairs on a large scale was first undertaken by the state apparatus of the United States of America and the United Kingdom, in selection and deployment of draftees (first other ranks, later officers), during the two world wars of the twentieth century. The primary focus of psychology was and is the individual; the assessment of various abilities, aptitudes and potential, delineating individual differences, using standardized tests and psychophysical measures, was the special province of the psychologist. Sociology with its subdiscipline of occupational sociology, also made systematic inroads into the study of a changing working environment, generating, at macro level, a body of knowledge, at times complementary, and at other times tangential to the prevailing transatlantic *Zeitgeist* of secular individualism.

Although Freud, with followers, antagonists, revisionists and others, had originated psychoanalytic psychotherapy at the turn of the century, this was practised by only a few, for the benefit of the emotionally disturbed. Counselling, at least as we know it today, did not appear on the scene until well into the twentieth century, and vocational guidance or career guidance for most of the time was a matching of people and jobs, by those who took on (for various reasons) the role of providing such guidance.

The matching procedure was also a reflection of the scientific status of psychology, professedly objective and 'value-free', employing statistical methods, and developing the technology, the instruments, and a plausible rationale for occupational guidance and placement. The German psychologist, Hugo Munsterberg (1913) who visited the USA in the late 1890s, spending some time at Harvard University, is said to have provided the impetus for developing a variety of measures to boost industrial efficiency, matching men and machines being among the most important.

Many historians of vocational guidance nominate Frank Parsons (1909) as the father of the vocational guidance movement. Although perhaps only indirectly influenced by Munsterberg, and himself not a psychologist, Donald Super (1983) describes Parsons as 'a Boston lawyer-engineer-social reformer who became interested in unemployed school-leavers and set up a *counselling* service in the Boston Civic House, a social settlement' (my italics). Although the word 'counselling' is obviously a post hoc description of what took place in career guidance in the early 1900s, the authors of *Career Guidance, Practice and Perspectives* (Gysbers *et al.* 1973: v) identified it as 'a reform movement – a movement dedicated to helping individuals meet the challenges of the social and economic changes taking place during that time. [Career guidance] was seen then as a single event [occurring] at a specific time'.

In his posthumously published book *Choosing a Vocation* (1909), Parsons had defined vocational guidance as an 'aid to young people in choosing an occupation, preparing for it, finding an opening in it, and building up a career of efficiency and success'. Parsons (1909: 5) elaborates the three-step procedure as follows.

> In the wise choice of a vocation there are three broad factors: 1) a clear understanding of yourself, your attitudes, abilities, interests, ambitions, resources, limitations and their causes, 2) a knowledge of the requirements and conditions of success, advantages and disadvantages, compensations, opportunities and prospects in different lines of work, 3) true reasoning in the relations of these two groups.

In the United Kingdom, since the 1880s, labour market bureaux had been intermittently operated by local authorities and charitable organizations, mainly as a welfare activity. Up to the end of the First World War, the generally held view was that any and all workers who wished to work could easily find it. Unrestrained market forces would eradicate unemployment. However, economic depression during the inter-war years created the misery of wide-spread unemployment in industrial societies, and resulted in the government adopting Keynesian economics for job creation and public works on a hitherto unprecedented scale.

Winston Churchill's Labour Exchange Act of 1909 empowered 'the Board of Trade to establish, take over and maintain labour exchanges' (Bradley 1990: 137). This is regarded as a landmark piece of legislation initiating a state manpower policy. The Act also established a network of separate Juvenile Employment Offices to serve the needs of the young. The Education (Choice of Employment) Act 1910 soon followed, permitting local education authorities to set up Juvenile Employment Bureaux, the precursor to today's Careers Service.

This division of responsibilities resulted in some confusion, where the Employment Offices registered vacancies, placed and reviewed progress of the young person (almost exclusively male in the early days) while the Employment Bureaux registered availability for work and provided vocational guidance. This arrangement, however unsatisfactory, existed until 1923 when all aspects of the service were handed over to the local education authorities or to the Ministry of Labour by default.

> By this time a system of transferring information had developed such that both the medical service and schools provided information to juvenile employment officers to enable them to give effective guidance. This covered the educational and medical background, an occupational recommendation by the teacher, an assessment of personality and a general report by the head-teacher. The information was entered on a *school-leaving card*, although its quality varied from school to school . . . An almost exact replica of this inter-war system exists today [with] its shortcomings . . . equally clear.
>
> (Bradley 1990: 139)

It has been said however, that the Youth Employment Service was in its inter-war period mainly concerned with the problems of those who had difficulties in finding work. Therefore, with the postwar boom, when wages and conditions became better, and demand for youth labour exceeded supply, the service was underused and almost became an irrelevancy, both in the eyes of the school-leaver as well as prospective employers.

It was not until the passage of the 1944 Education Act, with the school leaving age raised to 15, and the 1948 Employment and Training Act, with legal provision for youth up to the age of 18, that there began a very wide geographical coverage of the Youth (in place of Juvenile) Employment Service in Britain. The Employment and Training Act (1948) made provision for all schools to be required to furnish to the Youth Employment Service particulars relating to the health, ability, educational attainments and aptitudes of all children leaving school so that they might be given adequate 'advice and assistance'. Vocational guidance has become an integral part of education since then.

Meanwhile, industrial psychologists had established a reputation for their skill in resolving problems involving the productivity of factory workers. They had, for example, investigated fatigue among wartime munitions workers and demonstrated that reducing hours of work and improving working conditions helped to increase productivity. They took the credit for advancing simultaneously the twin goals of efficiency and welfare.

Perhaps it is worth asking whether there is an optimal amount of time spent daily working for a living? Csikszentmihalyi (1997: 10) has this to say:

> According to some anthropologists, among the least technologically developed societies, such as the tribesmen of the Brazilian jungles or the African deserts, grown men rarely spend more than four hours a day providing for their livelihood – the rest of the time they spend resting, chatting, singing, and dancing. On the other hand during the hundred years or so of industrialization in the West, before the unions were able to regulate working time, it was not unusual for workers to spend twelve or more hours a day in the factory. So the eight-hour workday, which is currently the norm, is about halfway between the two extremes.

PSYCHOLOGY AND WORK

The National Institute of Industrial Psychology (NIIP) was established in 1921 and continued the work begun by the Industrial Fatigue Research Board which had conducted research into the working conditions of munitions workers. The NIIP was a self-financing organization supported by politicians and progressive employers. It was founded by C.S. Myers, reputedly the first British experimental psychologist, whose early career was as a medical doctor. In a journal first published in 1922, the NIIP summarized its work under two headings, Investigations and Research, and Vocational Guidance and Selection.

The intellectual ferment of the time favoured the tried and tested methods of natural science with its emphasis on quantification as the dominant mode of investigation. This made inroads into almost all human sciences including sociology, politics, economics and anthropology. The greater the degree to which the experimental method and laboratory simulations were used, the more credibility and prestige these disciplines enjoyed. Since there was a visible hierarchy of sciences (with physics demonstrably the most successful), psychology began to emulate physics in seeking invariant laws of human behaviour.

While Galton in Britain had originated the process of measuring and quantifying human performance, especially reaction speeds (useful in information processing), Simon and Binet in France had measured the mental age or the differential learning potential of schoolchildren, a concept later famously operationalized as 'intelligence' and universally adopted by psychologists, although with the French authorities the procedure had been merely an 'administrative device'. Psychophysical measurement begun at Wundt's laboratory in Germany, added other 'scientific' tools to the armoury of the now burgeoning profession of practitioners in applied psychology. The statistical concept of the 'normal curve' when applied to human characteristics gave rise to the identification of individual differences along many dimensions that were elicited through the use of standardized tests. In vocational psychology, the matching of individual characteristics with the specific demands of a work role came to be known as the 'trait-and-factor' approach. Vocational guidance, and job design, was summarized in the phrases 'fitting man-to-the-job' (FMJ) and 'fitting job-to-the-man' (FJM).

To Cyril Burt, employed by the London County Council as its first educational psychologist in 1912, falls the honour of establishing the vocational guidance department of the NIIP in 1922, which he headed until 1924 (Hollway 1991: 62). He was instrumental in constructing selection tests for typists and shorthand writers, although he is better known for the introduction of the eleven-plus examination for sorting pupils into secondary modern and grammar school education. In keeping with the temper of the times, Burt was able to declare rather grandly that it is the duty of the community, first, to ascertain what is the mental level of each individual child; then give the education most appropriate to his [*sic*] level, and lastly, before it leaves him, to guide him into the career for which his measure of intelligence has marked him out.

(1924, quoted in Hollway 1991: 54)

In addition to intelligence and other measures of optimal performance such as sensory acuity and motor skills, measures of personality and interests were also developed. When in the Strong Vocational Interest Blank first appeared in the United States in 1927 (still extant as the Strong-Campbell Vocational Interest Inventory), it was hailed in a contemporary article entitled 'Vocational guidance is now possible' as a tool that at last enabled counsellors to match people to occupations. Reportedly the first standardized interest inventory was developed by the Bureau of Personnel Research at the Carnegie Institute of Technology (Fryer 1931: 66–9). Reproduced below in part, it makes for interesting reading. It tends to support postmodern deconstructions of knowledge production in the social sciences and gives the lie to the pretensions of value-free, objective, and 'scientific' status claimed for psychological research.

THE CARNEGIE INTEREST INVENTORY (1921 EDITION)

Part I – Choice of Occupations

Draw a circle around L if you would like doing that kind of work.

Draw a circle around D if you would dislike doing that kind of work.

Draw a circle around ? if you have no decided feelings toward that kind of work. Or know nothing about it.

Disregard any salary or social differences or any possible family objections.

Consider only your interest and satisfaction in doing each of the kinds of work listed. You are not asked whether you would take up the occupation permanently; you are merely asked if you would enjoy that kind of work.

Assume that you have the ability necessary for each of the occupations.

Actor .... L ? D
Architect .... L ? D
Artist .... L ? D

Astronomer .... L ? D
Auctioneer .... L ? D
Automobile Salesman .... L ? D
Auto racer .... L ? D
Auto repairman .... L ? D
Hotelkeeper or Manager .... L ? D
Judge .... L ? D
Labor Arbitrator .... L ? D
Lawyer .... L ? D
Librarian .... L ? D
Lighthouse tender .... L ? D
Locomotive Engineer .... L ? D
Machinist .... L ? D
Magazine writer .... L ? D

Part II – Likes and Dislikes

Draw a circle around L! if you like the item very much.
Draw a circle around L if you like the item.
Draw a circle around ? if you have no decided feelings toward
   the item.
Draw a circle around D if you dislike the item.
Draw a circle around D! if you dislike the item very much.

Fat men .... L! L ? D D!
Fat women .... L! L ? D D!
Thin men .... L! L ? D D!
Thin women .... L! L ? D D!
Tall men .... L! L ? D D!
Short men .... L! L ? D D!
Short women .... L! L ? D D!
Blondes .... L! L ? D D!
Chinless people .... L! L ? D D!
People with hooked noses .... L! L ? D D!
Cross-eyed people .... L! L ? D D!
Blind people .... L! L ? D D!
Deaf mutes .... L! L ? D D!
People whose eyes are set close together .... L! L ? D D!
Men who wear beards .... L! L ? D D!
Bow-legged people .... L! L ? D D!

The *Journal of the NIIP* for 1922 carried an extract from the *New York Times* (17.2.22) which extolled the virtues of psychological testing and quoted the test publishers, The Psychological Corporation, as believing 'that it would be possible to increase by $60 billion the national wealth of each year by properly fitting every man, woman and child [*sic*] to the kind of work each would best perform' (Hollway 1991: 56). It is interesting to note that a plan advocated by an NIIP luminary of the time, Muscio, was a large vocational laboratory for girls and boys about to become wage earners, under the control of psychologists, and connected with both schools and industry. Although both sexes were ostensibly equally catered for, it must be remembered that occupations at the time were largely segregated.

A thoroughgoing treatment of a piece of research on vocational guidance conducted in UK was published by Earles in 1931. It is instructive to reproduce the title and subtitle here. The book was entitled *Methods of Choosing a Career*, and its lengthy subtitle was, *A Description of an Experiment in Vocational Guidance Conducted on Twelve Hundred London Elementary School Children*. In his foreword, the Viscount d'Abernon as president and patron of the NIIP, and an obvious member of the 'leisure class', expresses fine sentiments about the book:

> I can commend it without hesitation to the many who must share my conviction that in more scientific vocational guidance lies one of our brightest hopes for the improved welfare of humanity ... Indeed, there can be no doubt that a large proportion of the unhappiness in this world must be attributed to individuals being engaged in occupations unsuited to their temperaments and their capacities.
>
> (Earles 1931: 7)

There was of course no means of assessing whether the tests used in vocational guidance research were valid and reliable. Such concepts were in their infancy. The tests developed for this research were of several kinds. There were nine short subtests of one-and-a-half to nine minutes' duration under the heading Group Test of Intelligence. Then there were nine more subtests in the clerical group with a supplementary test in grammar and spelling. A test of dictation was very similar to school tests of that period. There was also a test of visuo-spatial aptitude labelled Form Relations and Memory of Design. Children who took part were strongly advised to take up occupations recommended by the NIIP researchers based on test performance. Tenure in a job was regarded as sufficient proof of success in job-matching. While the authors list many provisos as to why the conclusions could not be seen as definitive, this is put down to the many practical difficulties in obtaining perfect data. It is not recognized as due to any deficiencies in methodology. It was nonetheless an influential and pioneering piece of work in applied psychology.

GUIDANCE FOR YOUNG PEOPLE?

Yet there was a difference in emphasis between the United Kingdom and the United States of America in the way vocational guidance for the young developed. At about the same time that Frank Parsons was articulating the world's first systematic theory of career guidance, there were others who independently introduced vocational guidance programmes in schools. Jesse Davis is credited with introducing the first of its kind at Grand Rapids, Michigan, in 1907. Soon school counsellors began to be appointed in several states on many Youth Service Programs.

The United States Employment Service (USES), which was created by the federal government during the Great Depression to stabilize the imbalance between labour supply and demand, took over and expanded the youth programme. In the United Kingdom, however, it was the Department of Labour that took the initiative in vocational guidance with school counsellors appearing very much later (see Mabey and Sorensen 1995). The Youth Employment Service and later the Careers Service have, throughout their existence, been considered 'outsiders' to the school system.

In 1924, when the UK government vested powers of vocational guidance with local education authorities, one of the earliest instituted under this legislation was the Birmingham Educational Committee. Two of the Birmingham Juvenile Employment Officers were trained at the NIIP, and between them, they were said to have produced six reports including industrial surveys (Hopson and Hayes 1968). Writing about the Birmingham Youth Employment Service of that period, Tony Newton commends its foresight in recognizing equal opportunity issues which in comparison appear to be deficient in today's Careers Service, since even the term 'equal opportunities' was not used until 1988:

> Every year there was a report to the Education Committee on the destinations data, in which the outcomes for young *immigrants* were compared in detail across all types of industry with those for the *host population*. Never mind the dated terminology (we all have to start somewhere), this was an opportunity to provide decision-makers with powerful material to challenge

employers, let the people know about the way in which unfair discrimination was operated, and give discriminated groups the ammunition to prove their points.

(1997: 30 italics in the original)

Providing information on occupations available in the locality, industrial visits for observation of work done by adults who may be seen as role models, work experience placements, providing information on employers and posting vacancies were all activities engaged in by the early youth employment officers. Much of this is still being carried on by the Careers Service, assisted to a varying degree by careers teachers and school counsellors. As Bradley (1990: 143) writes of all such activities:

> The fundamental aim of vocational guidance had been that of appraising and matching clients' abilities, aptitudes and interests with the requirements of jobs. The individual was regarded as possessing fixed vocational skills, and the approach essentially involved 'directing' the young person to the most suitable job as perceived by the youth employment officer. As a result, a single interview and talk at the end of a young person's educational career was seen as sufficient.

However, when 'developmental' theories of vocational choice emphasizing the self-concept and life stages of the individual began to replace the early 'trait-and-factor' theories in the 1950s, the careers education movement in schools gathered pace. Whereas in 1947–49 vocational guidance interviews conducted by the youth employment officers amounted to 767,340, in 1962–65 they had increased to a staggering 2,080,292 (quoted by Bradley 1990: 144).

One of the reasons for the decline of the trait-factor, also termed the differentialist approach to vocational guidance, was that a thoroughgoing, well documented longitudinal study of ex-US servicemen conducted by psychologists Thorndike and Hagen tended to question theories that linked vocational choice to psychological test results. The findings were reported in a book entitled *Ten Thousand Careers* (Thorndike and Hagen 1959) which became a classic in the vocational psychology literature.

One of the early researchers at NIIP, Alec Rodger, became the first Professor of Occupational Psychology (as vocational and industrial psychology came to be known in the United Kingdom), at Birkbeck College, University of London. He is credited with the introduction of the Seven Point Plan, 'a rough sketch of a scientifically defensible system for the assessment of occupational potential for both personnel selection and vocational guidance' (Rodger 1952; reproduced in Hopson and Hayes 1968: 359–73). The Seven Point Plan, which stemmed from the differentialist (trait-and-factor) viewpoint, was extensively used by the Youth Employment Service and its successor the Careers Service. Many large organizations used it as an interview protocol in employee selection. Information was gathered under the following headings, using psychometric tests where appropriate.

1 Physical make-up,
2 Attainments,
3 General intelligence,
4 Special aptitudes,
5 Interests,
6 Disposition,
7 Circumstances.

Meanwhile, research begun by Eli Ginzberg at Columbia University was continued by Donald Super, who has become an illustrious advocate for the developmental approach in vocational psychology. As stated earlier, the developmental notion of career choice highlights the limitations of a once-and-for-all decision to enter and remain in a job, as well as the notion that there are invariant, measurable attributes within the individual that fit him or her to a matching work role. Super's ongoing research resulted in his 'Life-Career Rainbow', which is a graphic portrayal of his life-span life-stage theory applied to a variety of life roles. It places the work role, or vocation, in the context of other life roles such as parent, or carer of ageing parents, which at certain times of one's life-career may be equally, or more important, than the role of worker.

The traditional approach had given rise to the 'square pegs in round holes' epithet to describe occupational mismatches. Whereas the differentialist approach vested power in the expert, who for the most part, espoused the values and demands of societal institutions of the state, commerce and industry, the developmental approach led to a more interactionist stance. In 1965, Hoyt in his Address to the Fifty-ninth Annual Vocational Convention at Miami Beach, Florida, could still emphasize that, 'guidance workers consider their function to be essentially one of helping people choose wisely from among the alternatives available to them'. However, he also cautioned that 'Congress, in making funds available for guidance and counselling, was thinking about manpower utilization objectives and not about the individual's right to lead his [sic] own life and choose his own occupation.' But, he added reassuringly 'social needs can best be met indirectly by meeting individual needs directly'.

Writing about changes in career education in schools during the late 60s in Australia, Morgan and Hart (1977: 3) say

[*It*] encourages students to think about themselves and the world of work simultaneously, over a long period of time, so that by the time careers decisions have to be made the student will have developed the necessary knowledge, understanding and skills with which to make an intelligent response.

Currently, there are as many theories of career decision making or vocational choice as there are research paradigms in psychology. These include psychodynamic (Roe, Bordin, Savickas), client-centred (Patterson, Cochran), behavioural (Krumboltz, Thoresen), social-learning (Bandura), and personal construct (Tyler), although the typology is somewhat arbitrary as some of the theorists listed who are still working in the field may see themselves as eclectic or evolving, with bridges constantly being built across theoretical boundaries.

Holland, who had developed a theory based on occupational personality types in the differentialist tradition in the 50s, has continued to enjoy popularity based on the fact that most of his postulates are amenable to empirical verification more easily than those of some of the other theories. Modest correlations have been reported. He is on record as having stated that it is possible to refine and streamline theories of vocational choice and fitness such that computer programmes could, in the future, take over the function of a vocational counsellor. Computer-assisted career guidance has so far, at least in the UK, been merely an adjunct to vocational guidance offered by professionals trained to a varying degree. It has not replaced careers advisers.

Keeping schoolchildren informed about the world of work had been the province of the careers teacher (so designated after brief in-service training) in secondary schools for several decades before school counsellors began to be trained in the 60s in Britain. Peter Daws (1976) chronicles the first decade of school counsellors trained at a few provincial British universities staffed by American Fullbright scholars who were invariably academics drawn from the fields of vocational and counselling psychology. Many of their functions were taken over in Britain by educational psychologists attached to the School Psychological Service, which developed later and more slowly than the School Medical Service, begun as far back as 1907. Counselling in the Rogerian non-directive manner was a new import that fitted well into the 1960s youth culture in Britain (Rogers 1951). According to Daws (1976), counselling and careers guidance diverged at that time, with school counselling becoming generic and more prestigious, with a longer academic training than career guidance training. The latter continued to be offered by the Department of Education and Science, through short in-service training courses.

The Ministry of Education Newsom Report *Half Our Future* (1963: 78), in referring to the work of a school careers adviser, had stipulated that

> there should be at least one member of staff whose special business is to be knowledgeable about employment and further education, to organise reference and display material, and to make the eventual liaison between school and parents, youth employment service and employment. It is important too that such a member of staff has a teaching programme which allows him [*sic*] to do these things.

The Newsom Report recommendations, implemented by the government, raised the school-leaving age to 16, and are said to have led to a more 'outward looking' approach to the school curriculum.

However, there is no mention of a counselling role for the careers adviser anywhere in the Newsom Report. School counselling, although 'founded and funded' through US vocational guidance concerns, became detached from its origins and moved more and more towards mental health issues. According to Daws (1976), it was the National Association for Mental Health which had been campaigning for early, school-age preventative interventions with the aim of reducing the incidence of disfunctionality in later life.

Daws (1976: 23), in describing the first one-year counselling courses for teachers as they were gradually extended to longer and more extensive courses writes:

> [I]n those early days, few people if any, would have defended the relegation of careers guidance to a minor place in counselling courses. Certainly, it was not part of the intentions of the American scholars who visited us. Yet it occurred. Part of the explanation, one suspects, being in the addictive attractions of the technique of client-centred counselling which found a more satisfying challenge in the problems of the distressed and the confused than in the apparently more straightforward and rational tasks of curricular and vocational choices. A further important factor was the inclination of the teachers to accord much less prestige to careers work than to work with disturbed and troubled children, just as the careers officer is seen as of more modest professional standing than the psychologist. There was quickly established a separation of 'careers' from 'counselling'.

Writing in 1958, Gilbert Wrenn, who as a Fullbright visiting scholar later taught and trained British school counsellors at the University of Keele, suggests that 'among psychologists, counselling psychologists had the lowest prestige among specialisms requiring a doctorate' (1958: 242). This was mainly because counselling psychologists were left with career guidance work, leaving the more prestigious mental health interventions to clinical psychologists with greater claims to the latter. One of the main reasons for such perceived differentials, it is believed, was that no adequate theory of vocational choice and development existed at the time, although it is debatable whether any real consensus exists even today.

It is also important to note that the British school context was changing. 'An important impetus to the acceptance of counselling by schools, was the movement towards comprehensive schools, which began contemporaneously with the counselling movement' (Daws 1976: 25).

Another blow to the scientific prestige of vocational guidance work in Britain was the demise of the National Institute of Industrial Psychology. Donald Super who exerted immense influence on the development of vocational guidance and counselling in the United Kingdom, both directly through his writings and indirectly through his many students working here, writes, 'The early pioneering and eminence of the NIIP did not continue, its research and development work ceased, and its contract work with industry was in due course not enough to keep it functioning in any way' (Walsh and Osipow 1983: 18). However, the NIIP was to a great extent replaced by

> a variety of researching university teachers in Counselling or in Occupational Psychology such as Barrie Hopson of Leeds, Richard Nelson-Jones of Aston, Peter Herriot at Birkbeck and Peter Warr of Sheffield, by training programs in the teaching-oriented poly-technics, and by institutes such as the National Institute of Careers Education (NICEC) in Cambridge that are more concerned with career development than with matching approaches.
> (Walsh and Osipow 1983: 18)

It is instructive to compare pre-war and postwar concepts of vocational guidance, first as officially defined by the American National Vocational Guidance Association in 1937, and a definition by Donald Super three decades later. The NVGA formulation runs '[I]t is a process of assisting the individual to choose an occupation, prepare for it, enter upon and progress in it', while Super refers to it 'as the process of helping a person to develop and accept an integrated and adequate picture of himself [*sic*] and of his role in the world of work, to test this concept against reality, to convert it into reality with satisfaction to himself and benefit to society'(Crites 1969: 21).

In 1973, the Department of Education and Science defined three objectives of careers education.

1 To help boys and girls to achieve an understanding of themselves and to be realistic about their strengths and weaknesses,
2 To extend the range of their thinking about opportunities in work and in life generally,
3 To prepare them to make considered choices.

These goals may be contrasted with four broad 'content domains from which student outcome goals and objectives . . . [are] devised' as identified by the University of Minnesota Career Guidance Counseling and Placement Project.

(a) self-knowledge and interpersonal skills;
(b) knowledge of the work and leisure worlds;
(c) career planning knowledge and skills;
(d) basic studies and occupational preparation.

(Gysbers *et al.* 1973: 30)

Much has been written about the development of careers education, guidance and counselling in schools in the United Kingdom, since according to the traditionalist position, these were activities directed at the young in preparing them for a point of entry into the adult world of work. The ideal – though this was far from reality – was that the individual once in his or her correct niche would prosper and advance, usually within a single organization, until the age of retirement.

GUIDANCE EXTENDED

It was therefore a lesson well learnt during the years of economic depression in the United States, that vocational guidance could not be limited to those entering the working world for the first time. Many adults were economically dislocated and unemployed at that time. The United States Employment Service (USES) acted as a clearing-house through which prospective employees with the right skills could be matched with the right employers.

Pioneering work had been undertaken at the University of Minnesota since the 1920s when it originated the Minnesota Mechanical Abilities Project. In 1931, a separate agency was formed as the Minnesota Employment Stabilization Research Institute (MESRI) to undertake large scale longitudinal research into vocational choice and adjustment especially among adults. According to Crites (1969: 6) one of the early MESRI projects:

> pursued three objectives to: (1) test various methods of diagnosing vocational aptitudes of unemployed workers; (2) provide a cross-section of the basic re-education problems of the unemployed; and (3) demonstrate methods of re-education and industrial rehabilitation of workers dislodged by industrial changes.

As a means of accomplishing some of these goals MESRI continued to develop aptitude tests. The United States General Aptitude Test Battery (which has undergone many revisions, but is still widely used) originated there. Under the aegis of the USES in the 1930s, MESRI surveyed about 25,000 employers and 100,000 employees, first to gather occupational information from extensive job analyses, second to develop 'measures of proficiency and potentiality', third to establish job equivalence schedules for the transfer of skills between jobs, and finally to write job descriptions and compile a *Dictionary of Occupational Titles* (DOT).

MESRI also collected data on the occupational capabilities of youth in cooperation with the American Youth Commission, organized Community Research Centres, and devised a coding system of entry jobs which became Part IV of the *Dictionary of Occupational Titles*.

The *Dictionary of Occupational Titles* has continued to be updated and published every two years since 1939. It now contains descriptions of over 21,000 job titles. The DOT and the *Occupational Outlook Handbook* (first edition, 1949) remain the two authoritative sources of occupational information to be published in the United States. For a brief period in the United Kingdom, the equivalent, *Classification of Occupations and Dictionary of Occupational Titles* (CODOT) flourished, but died a natural death in the early 1980s.

Rethinking Careers Education and Guidance, theory, policy and practice (Watts *et al.* 1996) has attempted to explore the development of careers guidance beyond secondary schools in the United Kingdom. Chapters 5, 6, 7 and 10 in that book deal respectively with careers work in schools, in further and adult education colleges, in higher education (universities), and in other settings.

SCHOOLS

Law (1996: 96), identifies three broad phases in the development of careers work in schools. The first pre-1960s phase was described as a 'supplementary service' restricted to ad hoc information giving and talent matching. Such activities were conducted independent of the curriculum by either the headteacher or by a designated careers teacher not specifically trained for the role.

The second phase was labelled an 'optional part of the curriculum'. It was manifest during the late 1960s and the early 1970s. The aim was to avoid inefficient individual guidance when this could be done more economically, and perhaps more effectively, by involving the whole class. Although contemporary planners envisaged careers education, guidance and counselling as a 'continuous process for all from the age of 13 onwards' (DES 1973), most secondary schools were able to provide a time-tabled careers lesson only in the last year of schooling. Grammar schools excluded themselves even from this scanty provision.

The DOTS model, as it came to be known, classified careers education and guidance under four headings: Decision learning (what will I do?), Opportunity awareness (where am I?), Transition learning (how will I cope?), and Self-awareness (who am I?). For the purpose of the acronym the order in which the participatory learning experiences are introduced into the curriculum has been scrambled. A more recent but irreverent acronym is SODIT where the 'I' stands for Implementation of plans!

The third phase, which Law (Watts *et al.* 1996: 98–9) terms an 'emergent requirement', surfaced in the late 1980s and continued into the 1990s. There were

> three, more or less, sequential attempts to move in the direction of mandatory provision, *targeted funding* (largely for pre-vocational work in schools); *policy imperatives* (from business, other interests and government); and *quality standards* (kite-marking schools that measure up to requirements)
>
> (original emphasis)

Under the banner of the 'new vocationalism', careers work became an integral part of the curriculum as never before. The Certificate of Pre-Vocational Education (CPVE) and the Technical and Vocational Education Initiative (TVEI) were introduced to cater for the less academically gifted 14–18 age group. The Youth Training Scheme which replaced the so-called temporary 'special programme' (the Youth Opportunities Scheme for unemployed school-leavers) depended upon the statutory Careers Service for its implementation augmented by centrally funded 'specialist careers officers'.

The Confederation of British Industry (CBI) (1993) argued for a better skilled workforce to ensure 'British competitiveness', proposing the entitlement to careers education, guidance and counselling to all school pupils from age 11 to 16. It also pressed, arguably with greater success, for closer links between schools and the business world. Agreement on criteria relating to quality standards is still some way off and is examined briefly in Chapter 5.

FURTHER EDUCATION

Hawthorn (1996a: 115) asserts that historically 'careers education and guidance was less well developed in further education than in other sectors of education'. Indeed it was the old Juvenile/Youth Employment Service that counselled the working-class lad with academic potential to take advantage of educational opportunities at 'night school' from which one strand of the present further education system evolved. One other strand included local authority residential colleges (teachers) and technical colleges. Daws (1976: 29) argues that the further education sector was 'spartanly endowed' with career guidance and counselling provision, partly because most students were 'occupationally-committed part-timers', and also because there was 'a tradition of impersonal work-related relationships between staff and students in technical education'.

However, during the late 1970s and early 1980s the number of 16–19-year-old students on non-vocational courses increased dramatically with considerable numbers also on pre-vocational courses that were not regarded as vocationally specific. Low-achieving participants were taking non-traditional routes to tertiary education, revealing their need for both educational and career counselling to be acute in the extreme. For example, the Department of Employment's Employment Training Scheme for adults, containing elements of career guidance and counselling to a varying degree, was also to a large extent the responsibility of the further education sector.

HIGHER EDUCATION

Watts (1996: 128) traces the history of university appointments boards which traditionally undertook on campus three main tasks of interviewing, information giving, and placing in jobs of undergraduates about to complete their degree courses. Often taking place in the spring term, these activities, later undertaken by prospective employers, popularly came to be known as the 'milk round'.

With the rapid proliferation of higher educational institutions beginning in the 1960s, the sedate appointments boards of Oxbridge gave way to highly professional in-house careers services. Unlike in secondary schools and in further education, in universities the teaching function and the counselling and career guidance functions tended to remain separate. As Watts points out, higher education is the only sector of education that is excluded from the 'statutory remit of the Careers Service answerable to the Secretary of State for Employment' (Watts *et al.* 1996: 388). This does not appear to have harmed the development of effective careers work in universities, although as Daws avers, it is strange that it took so long for universities to grasp the benefits of career counselling, since it 'fits more congenially the more mature, intelligent and verbal culture of tertiary education and the more equal relationships of staff and students' (Daws 1976: 29).

The first counselling service to be established at a British university was set up as an 'appointments and counselling service' at Keele in 1965. (The first single counsellor in a British university was employed in the School of Education at the University of Leicester in 1948. Keele provided the first *service* with more than one member of staff). However most other universities tended to separate the two functions of appointments (vacancy notification and vocational guidance) and personal counselling.

Computer-aided guidance systems were also introduced into higher educational institutions at this time. GRADSCOPE was developed as an interactive system. PROSPECTS (formerly ROGET) was said to have helped create an open-access approach to career guidance and counselling in higher education.

OTHER SETTINGS

Chapter 10 of Watts *et al.* (1996) is entitled 'Other sources of guidance on learning and work' (Hawthorn 1996b). Except for the mention of a few Employment Service programmes for the unemployed and similar initiatives by Training Enterprise Councils in England, no clear historical picture emerges as to the extent or development of what must be as yet a hidden, unsystematic and unrecorded area of activity. In this chapter, educational and vocational guidance/ counselling are conflated in what is essentially a discussion of a diffuse area of current theoretical and policy issues.

One influential theoretical development has, at least in the British context, been relevant and important. Roberts (1968), a British sociologist, put forward what he described as an alternative theory to the Super developmental, self-concept theory of occupational choice and development. He conceived of his theory as an opportunity-structure model, stressing the economic and social conditions of selection or self-selection to jobs and careers. He believed that educators and employers acted as gatekeepers, and that the stratification of the British social class system set limits to an individual's aspirations and exposure to models. He also believed that the concept of development was amenable to restatement in sociological terms, for example, as role theory and anticipatory socialization. Roberts tested several hypotheses said to have been derived from career developmental theory. These can be summarized as:

1 young persons' ambitions will gradually become more consistent with their jobs as their careers develop;
2 job satisfaction increases as careers develop; and
3 occupational mobility declines as careers progress.

According to Roberts, none of these hypotheses was unequivocally supported. (His sample consisted of 196 randomly selected youths between the ages of 14 and 23 living in a Greater London borough.)

The 1960s, when this study was undertaken, was a time of rapid economic growth and social mobility in the United Kingdom. Demand for unskilled and semi-skilled labour as well as routine office work exceeded supply, with wages rising rapidly. It is doubtful whether any global theory could have been adequately tested using such a small and attenuated sample.

The sample was divided into four categories: manual, non-manual, over three years in same job, and less than three years in the job.

One of the findings of this study was that 'ambitions do not determine careers but that careers determine ambitions'. Asking what jobs these youths aimed for before they entered the working world, and asking the same question after they had spent a couple of years in work, then comparing the two statements, hardly merits such a sweeping generalization. It is also a questionable assumption that the rate of vocational mobility, especially at a time of the Beatles and 'flower power', should be regarded as an indication of vocational maladjustment. Roberts (1968) concluded that the ideology of free vocational choice, axiomatic in the American theories, may not correspond to social reality of the United Kingdom. He may have had a point there.

That Donald Super, whose developmental theory was the one most under attack by Roberts, was not unaware of the societal and cultural influences on vocational choice is evidenced by his numerous references to such variables. For example, the following statement is found in a monograph he co-authored in 1957:

In selecting an occupation, the individual is influenced not only by personal psychological characteristics but also by multiple levels of social systems. These systems range from the direct influence of the home, school, and family, to community level variables (peer relationships, religious influences, social contacts), to the more general societal influences operating in American Culture (Macroinfluences).

(Super and Bacharach 1957)

It is curious, however, that nobody had realized that Roberts had been attacking a straw man, although Ben Ball (1984: 22) comes close:

The view put forward by Roberts 'that personal values are socially determined and dependent on opportunity structures' is useful for careers practitioners' understanding of client groups with special needs, for example the unemployed. However, it fails to explain satisfactorily how a client's values and aspirations can be translated into the search for rewarding work. Roberts' analysis cannot provide complete answers to the question all careers practitioners have at the back of their minds; 'How and why do different individuals undertake different kinds of work?'.

At the time, Roberts' vaunted demolition of the developmental theories of vocational identity and choice was regarded as a breakthrough. Yet his alternative opportunity-structure model could no more be operationalized than the theories he sought to replace. This is because, as Kline(1975) is at pains to point out, all theories of vocational choice and satisfaction, especially those of Ginzberg (1958; Ginzberg et al. 1951) and Super, are so general and wide-ranging as to be almost totally useless as predictive instruments. Kline, being a psychometrician, can in turn be accused of trying to fit the field of vocational guidance into a narrow and outdated paradigm.

Psathas (1968: 265), an American sociologist, appears to concur with Roberts' main thesis when he says:

it is likely that for large segments of the population, the concepts of vocational choice and development are simply not relevant as simple economic survival is a far greater occupational motivator than the implementation of [a] self-concept or some other idea of ego optimization.

On the other hand, he appears to parry Kline's attack successfully when he says that vocational guidance theories must be seen as general conceptual frameworks rather than articulated theory.

An important development affecting the future of counselling in careers guidance was the 1993 Trade Union Reform and Employment Rights Act which removed the statutory obligation of local education authorities to provide a Careers Service. It gave the Secretary of State for Education discretion as to how such a service is to be provided. Several different forms of service provision came into being, through competitive tendering and with public and private sector partnerships in specified local areas. Innovations and qualitative improvements were expected to follow, although constraints in funding and the need for income generation set the limits on their accomplishment.

Facing this challenge, The Institute of Career Guidance (ICG) set its stall in a leaflet entitled *Lifelong Career Guidance for Lifetime Career Development* (undated) as follows:

> Careers guidance is a process which enables individuals to acquire the skills they need to make choices and decisions about their futures. In helping individuals to clarify their options, careers guidance draws on skills which are best described by the seven activities of guidance developed by the Unit for the Development of Adult and Continuing Education (UDACE) – informing, advising, counselling, assessing, enabling, advocating and feeding back . . . It is the Institute's stated belief that all citizens should have access to guidance which is:
>
> * centred upon the individual;
> * impartial and unbiased, without pressure from planners and providers of opportunities;
> * confidential;
> * based on the principles of equal opportunities;
> * accessible to all potential users;
> * delivered by appropriately qualified staff.

This is a useful summary of the current position, upon which the chapters that follow can build, examining in greater depth the ramifications of the evolving theory and practice of career guidance and counselling, briefly outlined in historical context in this chapter.

· TWO ·

Counselling in careers guidance

From the foregoing discussion it may be concluded that careers guidance in one form or another has been a western European and North American phenomenon which developed over the best part of the twentieth century. This is largely true, and counselling, a rather recent form of intervention in human affairs, appears to flourish only in open, meritocratic societies that value freedom of choice and the autonomy of the individual. Counselling in careers guidance therefore may more often be seen in societies that are both technologically advanced and politically sophisticated.

Even among western democracies varying degrees of social stratification continue to exist due to historical reasons that tend to influence the range and effectiveness of formal guidance services. Echoing the sociological opportunity structure critique of occupational choice, Watts writes:

> Individuals tend to make choices within socially circumscribed limits, and are able to get much of the help they need from their family and informal networks. In societies with relatively high levels of social mobility, on the other hand, formal guidance assumes greater importance: individuals have a wider field of choice available to them, and their family and informal networks are less likely to provide informed help in relation to the full range of opportunities.
>
> (Watts *et al.* 1996: 371)

VARYING CONTEXTS

It is worth repeating that in individualistic, liberal-democratic societies careers guidance and counselling flourish in their most developed form. Tensions between societal needs and individual needs are never completely resolved even in these societies, but, as Watts (Watts *et al.* 1996: 370) points out, countries like Sweden with highly developed democratic institutions, manage, in guidance, 'a more radical process of ongoing social change'. Recognizing that individual choices could act as agents of change in society, Sweden's educational and vocational guidance providers actively aimed to develop a critical awareness of sources of information and influence and raise political awareness among pupils. Sweden's official policy statement on guidance issued as far back as 1971 'placed individual decision-making within a pluralistic social context in which issues of conflict and inequality were not to be avoided' (Watts *et al.* 1996: 370).

In contrast to the above, in the early 1990s the British New Right sought to bring in market principles to the delivery of guidance services. Careers services are now reconstituted careers companies, owned by a variety of organizations, including in England and Wales, private companies or training providers under contract to the Department for Education and Employment. In Scotland, similar services are run by a partnership between the local education authority and the Local Enterprise Councils.

> In England and Wales, each careers company may have different owners: sometimes a Training and Enterprise Council or Education Business Partnership may have joined with former careers service management to run the service, sometimes the service may be run quite separately from the TEC by another organisation . . . In yet other cases, the new careers company is simply the old management who made a successful bid to run the service themselves as a private limited company.
>
> (Lea 1997: 52)

These developments are echoed in countries like Australia and New Zealand, and to a lesser extent in the Netherlands.

Methods of assessment in recruitment and selection for jobs and careers in organizations also vary from country to country.

> Countries that are more universalist and achievement-oriented (e.g. the United Kingdom, North America and Australia) tend to use more objective criteria, which are measurable, such as intellectual abilities or technical skills, and so assess the ability

to satisfy technical task demands. More particularist, ascription-oriented countries (e.g. France and Italy) are more concerned with assessing whether the personality of the individual is likely to match the work group. Thus, for example, in France and Italy there is a tendency to use a number of interviews and interviewers. This is sensible if one believes that organizational success depends on the ability to function in a web of relationships and hierarchies.

(Anderson and Heriott 1997: 91)

To what extent a country's education system is geared to the needs of the employment system varies even among highly economically developed countries. For example,

the general content of French education, which emphasizes philosophy and Cartesian rationality . . . bears little relationship to actual job duties. In contrast, German education emphasizes employment opportunities beginning at the secondary level with clearly defined vocational training tracks for mechanical, technical, scientific and other occupations. The Dutch system, despite local variation, is a sort of middle ground emphasizing practical but generalist skills.

(Anderson and Herriott 1997: 29)

In France, work organization, in line with the educational system, is far more hierarchical than in most other industrialized countries. For example, attending a prestigious *grand ecole* is regarded as better than attending any other university, and almost certain to guarantee a top management position. Whereas in Anglo-Saxon cultures selection methods are based mainly on cognitive tests and the assessment of task competencies, in France and Italy, as hinted at earlier, more reliance is placed on interviews, personality questionnaires, and the assessment of interpersonal social skills. It is curious that where graphology is dismissed as unscientific in the United Kingdom and North America, it is extensively used as a selection device in France.

There are further differences in the organization of work and careers among the members of the European Union.

Both the Dutch and the French demonstrate the tight connection between education, culture and a social contract of work (albeit with distinctly different terms). Their nexus gives rise to opportunities for Dutch workers to bridge between different vocational tracks and creates for them employment stability. In France, it reinforces one's *cadre* or social standing but can reduce employability due to limits on inter-firm mobility and limited use of organization based learning.

(Rousseau and Tinsley 1997: 50)

However, in the postindustrial knowledge-based societies of the future, it is the quality of education of employees that is deemed to give commercial and industrial enterprises their competitive edge. In a country like Japan where differences between employees are played down, everyone strives to become a generalist, eschewing specialization. Most employees can take upon themselves to function adequately in any specialism. This is because of the high performance standards delivered by the educational system from elementary school to university. The system weeds out poor performers while the able rise to the top. Formal assessments are therefore not essential in hiring, as educational credentials are seen as valid in themselves. Most job applicants are put through repeated interviews, or informally assessed for organizational fit, through being invited to lunches and dinners by prospective bosses and co-workers.

It is customary to separate guidance into three main components as educational guidance, vocational guidance and personal guidance. Whether they are all to be offered within a single agency or separately depend on the historical conventions developed in each country. While in Germany there are clearly separate agencies assigned to each function, in Belgium, all three functions are brought together under one agency, the Psycho–Medico–Social Centre, although the roles themselves are kept distinct. In a country like Ireland, in contrast, all three activities tend to be undertaken by one school, or guidance, counsellor.

The most highly industrialized and developed societies are not immune to periods of economic depression and recession. Redundancies and lay-offs, first seen among the unskilled and the semi-skilled, have increasingly affected even the white-collar, managerial and professional ranks. This is seen as the result of increasing globalization of the world economy. While unemployment is painful and demoralizing enough for the adult, youth mass unemployment, where the young have been unable to establish themselves in any work role at all, takes on the magnitude of a social catastrophe. In such times, careers guidance and counselling can become a Herculean task.

STATE INTERVENTIONS

This was the scenario in the United Kingdom in the 1970s and early 1980s. The recession was said to have been exacerbated by

Thatcherite monetary policy of the day, which meant a cut in the rate of growth of the money supply, resulting in a high rate of unemployment insensitively ignored by the government as 'a price worth paying'. To compound the problem, there was also a bulge in the number of young people reaching school-leaving age at the time.

> Whereas in 1969–70 there were 691,000 school-leavers, by 1975–76 this had grown to 817,000, and the growth continued, to reach a peak in 1982–83 of 913,000. Competition for available jobs also intensified as a result of the increase in the married women's participation rate – resulting, for instance, in an extra million entering the labour force between 1971 and 1976. At the exit end of the labour force, fewer people were reaching retirement age because of the slump in births in the 1914–18 period. As a result, the number of young people searching for work at careers offices swelled considerably.
>
> (Bradley 1990: 146)

More and specialized careers officers were recruited and trained, whose main purpose was to channel the youth into government initiated Special Employment Measures, such as the early Job Creation and Work Experience programmes. Since these programmes came into being in a rather fragmented way, and did not have the desired effect of reducing youth unemployment, the government introduced a national scheme aimed to give all 16–18-year-olds work experience as well as basic training. This began as the Youth Opportunities Programme in 1978 which five years later became the Youth Training Scheme. Only a small extra allowance was paid so that remaining on unemployment benefit was not made too attractive for those who would enter further education. According to Bradley (1990: 147), the work of 'submitting, placing, reviewing trainee progress and meeting guarantees set by the MSC (Manpower Services Commission) . . . placed considerable pressure' on the Careers Service, which, as Bradley testifies, it was able to cope with admirably.

A new qualification framework of work-based National Vocational Qualifications (NVQs) and 'applied' but education-based General National Vocational Qualifications (GNVQs) in addition to the traditional GCSE, GCE O and A levels had been introduced. The new qualifications are all regarded as equally valid as entry level qualifications for further, higher and professional education and training.

Youth Training, Youth Credits, and New Apprenticeships are recently developed schemes for the 16–17 age group with extensions up to age 18 for those with 'special needs', with training available to age 25. This appears to be an almost belated recognition by the United Kingdom government that to be competitive in a global economy in the twenty-first century, a skilled and trained workforce is an essential prerequisite.

Bradley (1990: 154) concludes that through the twentieth century the Careers Service in Britain

> has been shaped by, and has responded to, external events, especially those in the field of education and the labour market, as well as changes in theories of vocational guidance, legislation, economic policy and economic orthodoxy . . . this is not to be seen as a weakness . . . [but] . . . a testimony to its adaptability and durability.

The modern Careers Service is scrutinized a little more closely and candidly towards the end of the chapter.

THE LABOUR MARKET

Whatever the reasons, whether it is technological advance or global competition, among many other variables, the effects on the labour markets in the United Kingdom and other industrialized countries are similar.

> For many people working lives are less predictable and more fragmented. Some phenomena which contribute to this are labour flexibility, project work, speedy obsolescence of skills, and a consequent need for lifelong learning, job insecurity (perceived or actual), and increased workload and pressures for short-term performance.
>
> (Arnold and Jackson 1997: 429)

Historically, the employment market in the world economy was classified under three broad *sectors*. These have been labelled by economists as the *primary* and utilities sector, which include agriculture, fishing, mining, energy and water supply, the *secondary* sector, consisting of engineering, manufacturing and construction, and the *tertiary* sector, which covers all public services including health and education, distribution/transport, communications, hotels and catering, and business with miscellaneous services including banking, finance and insurance. In the United Kingdom, it is the *Standard Industrial Classification* (SIC) that is the official index of classification of sectors of employment.

Sectors are said to be useful in careers guidance as they appear to relate to popular classifications of jobs and to the awareness of the existence of major employers in each sector. There may be similarities in the types and patterns of work within each sector and a common culture built on these. Employment forecasts are invariably based and distinguished by sector, although, some occupations may be found across sectors that are fairly similar (see Hirsh *et al.* 1998).

With ongoing industrialization and continuous technological advance, the proportion of the population employed in the different sectors of a country's economy shifts from the primary sector, through to the secondary sector and moves on towards the tertiary sector.

At the beginning of the nineteenth century, employment in the UK was divided just about equally between the three sectors. By 1993, employment in the primary and utilities sector had fallen to under 4% of the population. In the secondary sector the proportion rose to well over 50% of the total by 1951. It remained relatively steady until the early 1960s but has since declined, and by 1993 was barely a quarter of the workforce. Tertiary sector employment has continued to expand proportionately throughout the period to almost 72% of the total by 1993.

(Lea 1997: 2)

The United States Secretary of Labour has categorized jobs in the US economy as, 1) symbolic-analytical services, 2) routine production services, and 3) in-person services (Savickas and Walsh 1996: 37). While the first category of job is increasingly available in developed economies like the United States and is valued and rewarded highly, jobs in the second and third categories get scarcer and are 'exported' to the less developed countries.

Although the terms work and career are almost synonymous for most people, these terms are variously employed by theorists in the field. An examination of concepts related to work, careers, jobs and occupations therefore cannot be overlooked as a means of comprehending the context and the complexities of careers guidance and counselling. *Webster's Dictionary* defines work as a verb:

to exert oneself physically or mentally for a purpose, especially in common speech, to exert oneself thus in doing something undertaken for gain, for improvement in one's material, intellectual condition, or under compulsion of any kind, as distinct from something undertaken for pleasure, sport, or immediate gratification.

A rather awkward but exhaustive description of what work means today is given by Edgar Krau (1997: 15):

Work comprises all activities undertaken in order to produce or to facilitate the production of material goods and to render services to human society, on the condition that this activity be recompensed with a certain fee and that certain rules regarding quantity and quality standards as well as an obligatory time and duration of the performed activity be observed. These conditions are important in order to differentiate between work and hobbies or play, in which the activities are performed without any imposed standards and with no expectation of fees. While work entitles people to a material remuneration, their reward may in addition consist in their advancement to a higher position, in an increase of competence or social power, or in the mere interest arising out of the content of work . . . [W]ork links together economic and technological, social and psychological aspects.

Although theorists and practitioners in careers guidance would tend to agree with Krau, they are also aware that there is increasingly less chance for most people for 'advancement to a higher position' and could question the need for an 'obligatory time and duration', especially for the growing numbers now working from their own homes.

Krau asserts that work and employment may not necessarily be the same thing but that for most people the two coincide. For him work therefore takes on the meanings associated with the word 'vocation'. For many, even those engaged in humdrum activities, he says, work offers the best chance of 'self-realization'. Work is therefore not just a collection of activities, but more importantly, social roles that confer varying degrees of social status. While work has been defined as the exercise of potentialities, career guidance is seen as the exploration of potentialities of the self in society. Work is a basic human activity that may not necessarily coincide with paid employment, as noted above. A somewhat idealized account of work states that it is concerned with *'agency'*, 'the endeavour to assert oneself, to initiate and influence events on the basis of planning ahead in accordance with one's view of the future as well as one's memories of the past' (Krau 1997: 17, quoting Fryer 1986).

JOBS AND CAREERS

In popular use the word career means advancement or progression in any sphere of activity and is often associated with the metaphor of climbing a ladder. Traditionally prestigious occupations requiring long and arduous preparation like law, medicine, the church, and the commissioned ranks of the military services have well defined career rungs. Organizations with management structures like central or local government and others modelled on military hierarchies also have careers that span from say, office boy or shop floor worker, to managing director or the chief executive officer. As discussed earlier, increasingly the flatter hierarchies in commercial and industrial organizations nowadays offer fewer opportunities for upward mobility. Continuing investment in lifelong learning and skill acquisition is usually required even to hold down one's current job or position.

While a career is viewed as a sequence of occupations, jobs and positions throughout a person's life, occupations are defined as groups of similar jobs across organizational structures. A job or position is a group of tasks or set of activities performed by one person utilizing skills, competencies and qualifications for that job. The term occupation is said to denote the duration, or time occupied in the pursuit of that occupation. Whereas the word career connotes a personal orientation of individuals having careers in and across occupations, the word 'occupation' appears impersonal, belonging more to the organizational world of job descriptions and job titles.

In the United Kingdom, the *Standard Occupational Classification* (1995) (SOC) is used to present employment data. This classification system groups occupations by similarity of qualifications, skills and experience. It places all occupations within nine broad groups. They are:

- managers and administrators;
- professional;
- associate professional and technical;
- clerical and secretarial;
- craft and related;
- personal and protective services;
- sales;
- plant and machine operatives;
- other.

However, with continuous change in the labour market, not just job titles and descriptions, but also task characteristics and worker attributes become obsolete very quickly, and the SOC is therefore not necessarily a convenient tool usable by careers counsellors.

Work is not always undertaken within large, aggregated formal enterprises, but could be done by oneself as the increasingly large group of self-employed individuals attests. Some of this type of work, which is undertaken part-time and possibly developed out of hobbies and pastimes, has been described as the 'mauve economy' (Handy 1984). This is in contrast to the ubiquitous 'black economy' which is any money earned without incurring liability to pay income tax. This type of work is often done by those with regular jobs who are said to be moonlighting when they engage in 'cash-in-hand' work.

The 'grey' or 'communal' economy, where work is done for oneself and others but is not paid for, is said to be over 50 per cent of the total amount of work done in most economies (Rose 1983). Since some of the work is done for others on the basis of friendship, good neighbourliness and reciprocity, it is said to strengthen social bonds and community ties (Argyle 1990). In periods of high unemployment this kind of work is organized locally on an exchange basis using a voucher system (for example, as seen in the Midlands during times of recession).

Careers guidance counsellors have become aware of these and many other variants of the once-only chosen, regular lifetime job with career advancement myth or ideal, of much of the orthodox career theory and practice. Even the distinction between employment and unemployment has begun to blur. Paid sabbaticals are no longer the preserve of the academic élite. They are offered to key workers in those knowledge-based enterprises usually with proportionately large research and development budgets. For varying reasons a company may second a senior executive to take up work for a fixed period with a charitable organization. Others retire early and dedicate themselves totally to voluntary, charitable work. Flexible working hours, job sharing, telecommuting, working reduced hours, working in a less demanding, or junior job when skills become obsolete, balancing leisure activities and paid work in unique ways, are all departures from the established norm, so that now 'we cannot turn back the clock where work and working practices are concerned' (Clutterbuck and Hill 1981: 18).

Whereas the opportunity structure theorists of the 1960s were concerned with limits to career choice imposed by societal structures like the class system, in the 70s and 80s limits embedded in issues of gender, ethnicity, disability and age have come to the fore. Most western societies have enacted legislation attempting to secure equal opportunities in removing artificial barriers to the participation of non-mainstream groups fully in the social and economic activities of communities of which they are a part. Societies can no longer risk the possibility of talent going to waste simply due to unexamined prejudice.

FUTURE TRENDS

In speaking of a 'new set of realities' and trends that could affect the future development of theory and practice in career guidance and counselling, Edwin Herr (1994) lists the following, which when abbreviated and adapted to the United Kingdom, neatly summarizes the contextual concerns of this chapter. Herr is however, careful to point out that the list does not 'exhaust the many possibilities that could be cited' (1994: 15):

- the globalization of the workforce (e.g. cross-national mobility and problems of cultural identity);
- a growing global labour surplus (e.g. voluntary work or leisure activities for those who may never be employed or re-employed);
- organizational transformation in the workforce (e.g. flattened hierarchies, matrix management);
- the rise of a contingent workforce (e.g. contract workers with special skills purchased for limited periods);
- the rising importance of the knowledge worker and of literacy, numeracy, communication and computer literacy (e.g. lifelong learning, problem solving and higher order thinking);
- linkages between positive or negative career experiences and mental health, self-esteem, purposefulness, physical well-being, the ability to support a family, and a perception of self-efficacy;
- new government policy and legislation on the school-to-work transition and work-based learning (e.g. modern Apprenticeships, GNVQs, New Deal and Welfare to Work);
- the demographic trends related to new entrants to the workforce, primarily women, ethnic groups and relocating EU citizens (e.g. the impact of cultural diversity in the workplace and cross-cultural interventions).

Although Herr is more concerned with addressing the vexed issue of the convergence (or lack of it) between career theory and practice, his conclusions regarding the importance of contextual factors in careers guidance and counselling are both convincing and timely and are worth reproducing here:

> [O]ne of the major emerging issues that will likely affect the convergence of career theory and practice relates to whether the construction of career theory continues to rest primarily on psychological assumptions about the primacy of individual action or on dynamic and interactional sociological, anthropological, organizational or economic perspectives that put people

into contexts that shape or restrict individual action and create barriers and obstacles that must be understood and surmounted. Such views give particular attention to the specific features of the context within which the individual is developing and with which she or he is engaged in adaptive changes . . . To the degree that such views become more fully embedded in career theory, they stimulate the development of interventions that are targeted not only to the individual but also to the family, the community, institutional settings, and social policy. Both from the perspective of career theory and practice, it is important to know the effects of institutional variables – family history, home community, socioeconomic status, race, ethnicity, gender – on career development and on the interventions appropriate to people experiencing different combinations of such contextual effects.

(Herr 1994: 28)

THE CAREERS SERVICE

The above list summarizes the central themes that run through the whole of this book, although in the United Kingdom, a recurring criticism is that recognition of contextual issues alone has not resulted in the concomitant growth of institutions or mechanisms to deliver the desired outcomes. Where individual initiatives have faced up to the challenge, these have been patchy and ephemeral due to problems of continuity of funding and retention of personnel.

The most up-to-date legislation covering the provision of careers education and guidance is the Education Act 1997. An important departure from previous practice is that under the Act (Section 43), all pupils in Years 9 to 11 in publicly funded secondary schools are *entitled* to careers education. This is expected to be delivered separately through time-tabled lessons as well as through cross-curricular (e.g. as part of personal and social education) and extra-curricular (e.g. work placement, visits to employers) activities. Pupils are expected to develop generic skills in decision making, negotiating, action planning and self-presentation, which are believed to contribute to preparing for adult life.

Schools are required to participate in building a Partnership Agreement with the Careers Service (Section 44) which has the major responsibility for the guidance element, including the provision of 'impartial' vacancy information to enable the young person to make educational or vocational choices. The careers adviser is the representative of the Careers Service while the careers coordinator is the lead teacher responsible for careers education at the school.

While *careers education* aims to provide young people with general information, knowledge and experience of job, training, further and higher education and the world of work, *careers guidance* is the process by which the young person is enabled to apply the skills, techniques and information at an individual level and so to make a realistic choice and appropriate decision about future options.

Apart from introducing the use of the careers library, the provision of which is another statutory requirement for schools, the careers adviser or advisers are required to allow drop-in facilities to the pupils, hold group discussions at the school itself, and hold individual guidance interviews with each pupil who requests it. The Department for Education and Employment publication explaining how the provisions of the 1997 Act apply in secondary schools stipulates: 'To protect both young people and careers service staff from any suggestion of impropriety, the room (where interviews are held) should be capable of being supervised by school staff' (DfEE 1997b: 16). Moreover, a parent or parents may be present at interview.

The interview (singular) is probably the only occasion during which any intervention resembling counselling could take place. However, as already alluded to, there is no mention of counselling anywhere in the Education Act 1997, or, except in passing, in any of the explanatory documents produced by the DfEE. The quoted sentence above shows how prescriptive and legalistic the whole enterprise of careers guidance in the UK has become. As a further example, paragraph 3 of Annex F, in the above document can be cited: 'People with disabilities (including learning disabilities) remain in the statutory group until they are settled in their career intention' (DfEE 1997b: 36). This smacks of the old-fashioned, trait-factor, once in a lifetime, right job belief system, where 'counselling' was no more than advising and directing someone to the job or career assumed to be the best possible fit under the circumstances.

An Institute of Manpower Studies (1994) publication neatly summarizes the work of the Careers Service in paragraph 1.2.2 'A wide ranging service', as follows:

There is more than one aspect to most services provided by the Careers Service. Thus 'careers guidance' for example, is a wide-ranging service embracing the provision of information, guidance and advice. These may be delivered in a written form, in face-to-face interviews and/or in group sessions. An action plan or statement of guidance may be produced for the user. For some, the main point of guidance is a fairly narrow focus on further education options, or getting a job or training place. In other cases, it is a less instrumental process concerned with stimulating new ideas and decision-making. The service could be delivered within school or college or at the Careers Service premises or at some intermediate venue.

(Hillage 1994: 5)

Where is the much vaunted 'counselling' offered by the Careers Service in the above? The IMS report quoted above gives an impressive list as constituting Careers Service Customers (1994: 6). In addition to the *young people* referred to ubiquitously, there are other *members of the statutory group*, who may be adults in full-time education or part-time vocational education outside the higher education sector, or people with 'special needs'. Some Careers Services choose to offer services to *adults* (increasingly for a fee), who may be categorized as those in work, those out of work, and those outside the labour force seeking entry or re-entry (e.g. women returners). The Careers Service must also ensure that the *parents* and guardians of young people (under 18) 'are aware of the services on offer and are encouraged and enabled to offer informed support to the careers decisions of the young people in their care'. Careers Services provide a range of services to *schools and colleges* including help with developing vocational elements of the curriculum (e.g. work experience placements); assistance with careers education delivery; provision of careers information; promotion of education business links and the collection and dissemination of destination statistics. Careers Services provide a vacancy notification service to local *employers* and provide the community with labour market information and developments in the educational field. It also provides a similar service to *training providers* including matching clients to available training opportunities. Increasingly, careers services work in partnership and/or under contract to other *labour market agencies* such as Training Enterprise Councils and Education Business Partnerships to provide a designated service. In such circumstances the agency may be the paying customer but the user may be a young person or a training provider. Lastly, the *community* at large relies on the Careers Service to provide an efficient, economic and effective service in terms of the labour market and the development of a lifelong learning culture.

The DfEE document, giving examples of 'good practice', cites a careers coordinator in a special school for pupils with physical disabilities as commenting:

There is a big difference in CEG [Careers Education and Guid-
ance] for special needs pupils – it's not identifying what pupils
can do but how pupils can be empowered to fit in with opportunities available. *Counselling skills are very necessary for work with
our pupils – I had a day's course a long time ago* – but such skills
are very important.

(DfEE 1997a: 22; my italics)

Curiously enough, nowhere is it acknowledged that careers coordinators should receive training in counselling. Neither has the writer
of the DfEE publication picked up and elaborated on the value of
counselling training to careers coordinators. Presumably, tutors and
teachers are expected to muddle through somehow.

In a 134-page NFER report entitled *The Role of the Careers Service in
Careers Education and Guidance in Schools* (Morris *et al.* 1995) based on
empirical research, the word counselling occurs in three places only,
but as something that the Careers Service provides as a matter of
course. On pages 4–5 the authors write somewhat blandly: 'schools
could draw upon careers officers' one-to-one counselling and guidance skills to enhance their own guidance work with young people'.
On page 12 they speak of 'Individual careers counselling and interviewing' as a component of careers guidance, and on page 45, they
claim 'some careers service staff were eminently qualified to provide training [to teachers] in the use of software packages or in one-
to-one counselling'. In the body of the report though, it is clear that
what is described as 'counselling' happens to be the one interview,
or at the most two interviews that the careers officer devotes to
some pupils. What goes on in the interview itself is only obliquely
referred to.

Although the requirement for parent contact is enshrined in
legislation, in practice 'mechanisms were rarely in place for teachers
to refer parents to the careers officer' (Morris *et al.* 1995: 53). Here,
individual initiatives rather than prescription appears to have won
the day. Even so, the questionable level of counselling sophistication on the part of careers officers is almost unwittingly revealed in
the following quotation:

> The practice of inviting parents to guidance interviews had gen-
> erally been discontinued, with officers finding that parents
> tended to dominate the interview or change the nature of the
> interaction with the young people. Parents were usually noti-
> fied of the interview and occasionally invited to the latter part
> of it or to a discussion with the careers officer at a later date,
> although take-up of such invitations were reported to be slight.

There was some interesting individual practice, such as the careers officer who was involved in a series of school-based 'hands-on' workshops for parents (they covered such topics as computer guidance software and work experience), or the careers officer who contributed regular articles to a newsletter which went home to parents.

(Morris *et al.* 1995: 53)

Most of the time there is the suspicion that careers officers or advisers merely report what they are expected to do, since most of their duties appear to be closely prescribed. For example, it is instructive to read Action Note 6, *Good Practice in Career Action Planning* (DfEE 1998a: unpaginated). The 'good practice' has reportedly been identified during Performance Assessment Surveys. Although the writer includes the disclaimer that the Note is not contractually binding, he or she also insists that 'the Department strongly recommends careers services to implement the good practice outlined'.

Under the heading 'Parents and Career Action Planning' there is very broad advice running to six paragraphs (15–20), some of it not entirely unambiguous. Paragraph 15 states:

In general parents should be invited to attend their child's career guidance interview. Young people, however, may not wish their parents to attend. Some careers advisers are positive in their view of the effect of parents on the guidance process, including the interview. They say it is helpful for clients to consider their parents' expectations when making career decisions because without parental support it would often be difficult for young people to do what they want.

(DfEE 1998a)

Paragraph 17 continues:

Careers advisers need to check parental expectations and manage these in the interview. If parents want to take an active part, advisers can keep the focus on their clients by telling parents what will happen in the interview. It is often helpful to leave parental involvement until after their children have made their own career intentions clear and then invite them to make comments or ask questions at appropriate points.

(DfEE 1998a)

In these extracts one sees the legal and contractual nature of what goes on in careers education and guidance such that one begins to wonder whether it is a professional and 'impartial' activity at all. Paragraph 18 is even more instructive in that it seeks to lay down, in sequence, what looks like an 'idiot's guide' to a simplified form of counselling. The writer appears to be unaware that it is palpably idiotic both to prescribe, as well as to attempt to follow slavishly, any such generalized, 'counselling-by-numbers' blandishments as the following:

18 When parents raise contentious issues advisers can help to resolve differences of opinion by engaging them actively in the search for a solution which balances different outlooks. To do this they need to:

- encourage everyone to give their points of view plainly;
- relate the issues in a way that everyone accepts;
- invite them to view things from other people's perspectives, for instance, teachers' or employers';
- challenge inaccuracies and misunderstandings on either side, for example those which confirm stereotyping and which depress realistic aspirations;
- look at the effect of going down different routes; and
- identify any areas of agreement on which practical actions can be built.

(DfEE 1998a)

It is even more instructive to read extracts from the Executive Summary of a survey on *Young People's Views of Careers Education and Guidance at School* (DfEE 1998d) where the overall conclusion was that young people 'generally lacked a clear concept of careers education and guidance'. This may be a tall order for youngsters who 'were often inarticulate and spoke in code', but their views of the 'bits and pieces' they reportedly experienced as CEG, are most informative.

- *Self-awareness activities* attracted some of the most negative reactions. The participants often did not like, or feel confident in, discussing their strengths and weaknesses in front of others and could not see how these activities linked in with making career choices. The unmediated use of computer print-outs full of apparently strange job suggestions, attracted frequent comment.
- Young people were keen to have a comprehensive range of *careers information*. They were concerned that:
  - the information given to them was being restricted and not always objective, particularly regarding study opportunities at college and vocational training routes as Modern Apprenticeships;

- it was not always up-to-date;
- information was not always presented in attractive or accessible ways, with too much written material. They welcomed
  opportunities to research careers information for themselves
  but requested more help from teachers and advisers to help
  select relevant data;
- problems in gaining ready access to computers, together with a
  lack of skills by their teachers and themselves, restricted their
  use of IT-based methods (including the Internet) to research
  information for themselves.

- *Guidance interviews* were much valued although they attracted
  mixed commentary. Young people felt that they:

  - worked best when the adviser was someone they knew and
    trusted, listened to them, and was responsive to their changing
    career preferences;
  - worked worst where they were poorly prepared for the inter-
    view and the adviser was unknown to them, had preconceived
    ideas about what they should do, did not engage in a two-way
    discussion and did not appear to provide objective advice.

This feedback hardly describes the sort of 'careers service staff
. . . eminently qualified to provide training . . . in one-to-one counselling'. The young people questioned also 'felt that CEG was tainted
by association with Personal and Social Education (PSE), which
they often held in low esteem and also felt that it lacked status in
the school' (DfEE 1998d).

A national survey of careers education and guidance was published in October 1998. In the sample were 148 secondary schools,
55 special schools and 10 special units (for excluded pupils). Referring to only secondary schools, the survey concludes that 'the majority of young people get a good deal from their careers education and
guidance' (Robb 1998: 3). The conclusions on special schools and
units were not so sanguine. However, even the 'good deal' which
the secondary schools were supposed to have enjoyed are given
in the most general and halo-inducing terms, while the criticisms
are more detailed and pointed. Again, counselling of any kind is not
dealt with anywhere for the benefit of readers of the survey report.

Positive features of CEG in secondary schools are listed as:

- ninety per cent of careers interviews were satisfactory or better;
- Year 11 Action Plans are 'sound and frequently good';
- careers teaching was satisfactory in 80 per cent of schools;
- attainment was satisfactory in 70 per cent of schools;

- good relations were seen between schools and career services;
- students demonstrated positive attitudes.

Overall criticism is voiced constructively in the form of a global imperative: 'Schools need to work with careers companies and the DfEE to raise standards to an acceptable level for all students' (Robb 1998: 3). However more detailed criticism is devastating and echoes the young people's criticisms reported above:

- the lead teacher may not have had access to training – only 30 per cent of careers coordinators have a relevant qualification;
- fifty per cent of staff teaching careers education were insufficiently trained;
- the careers lesson may be unchallenging in content and style;
- the careers library may be inaccessible or poorly maintained (one in 10 schools);
- careers lessons may not make connections to the rest of the curriculum or the RoA process (Record of Achievement – renamed Progress File);
- the timing of careers work (lessons and interviews) may not match pupil need because of the PSE (Personal and Social Education) structure or the interview schedule;
- parents may not be enabled to play a full role in supporting their daughter or son.

At system level, the survey is said to have identified a development agenda for the future. This is subsumed under four broad headings: curriculum; training; managing careers work; and partnerships. Lifelong learning and social inclusion agendas are also said to be important from the point of view of the present Labour government. Careers education and guidance have a part to play in delivering the outcomes of raising levels of achievement across the board. It seems strange that there has been no mention anywhere of individual assessment (not necessarily program evaluation) let alone individual counselling, which has been at the heart of careers guidance in the past in the United Kingdom (see Chapter 1). It is a strangely denuded and barren landscape that one encounters when delving into the public arena of counselling in careers guidance. The conclusion is inescapable that there is no such thing as counselling in careers guidance!

Morris, Simkin and Stoney (1995) during their empirical study of the Careers Service identified three models of careers education and guidance practice in secondary schools. They give detailed case studies in support of their models. Of the majority of schools, two-thirds practised the pyramidal model, one in six practised the parallel model, and 'less than one in six' practised what they called the guidance community model. Of the three, the parallel provision was the least effective. In this model:

> careers education was seen as the province of teachers in the school (although it might not be given much attention) while guidance primarily took the form of a careers service interview. In rare instances, some school staff additionally took on that role. In the most basic cases, there was little interaction or flow of information between the three key players in the guidance triangle: the careers officer, the coordinator and the young person or client. Little or no information about the young person was passed on to the careers officer, while the young people in turn received little or no prior information about the reason or purpose of the interview. The written outcome of the interview, even if passed to the school as well as to the interviewee played no part in the continuing further education of the student within the school.
>
> (Morris *et al.* 1995: 86)

The authors describe pyramidal provision as follows:

> In the second model, the interview was seen as the culmination of the guidance process, with the school and the careers service sometimes working fairly separately towards this event, but with a better interchange of information. In this more widespread model, the careers service was often involved in providing some factual input to the curriculum, support for the careers library and occasional INSET for tutors. Young people were better prepared for the interview than in the parallel provision model. Information about the young people, obtained from vocational questionnaires and/or staff reports was passed to the careers officer in sufficient time to have been of use in planning the interview. A written outcome of the interview was passed back to both the young person and the school, although it rarely played any part in continuing careers education. Further careers service interventions, such as referral or placement, were conducted on an individual basis, with the young person, in effect, becoming a personal client of the service after the interview had taken place.
>
> (Morris *et al.* 1995: 89)

The guidance community model as identified by the authors was able to promote 'the idea of careers education and guidance as part of a strategy aimed at life-long learning in which all stakeholders played a role' (Morris *et al.* 1995: 91).

The third model saw careers officers more actively involved in curriculum planning and review, sometimes as consultants, sometimes as part of a guidance team in the school. Young people were involved in skills development and action planning at an early stage in their school career and came well prepared to the guidance interview. Careers officers, in turn, were provided with detailed information about the interests, abilities and career aspirations (when known) of the young people who were coming to interview. The interview itself was seen as part of the educative process, and young people returned from interviews (often more than one) with ideas to research and follow up, before completing an action plan that led to transition. Feedback from the interviews was also passed on to school staff and informed future curriculum development (for example highlighting concepts or skills that might need to be enhanced for the individual or in the careers education programme in the school). In addition, a network of adults other than teachers from the local employer and training community and other bodies were actively involved in a wide variety of activities within the broader careers education curriculum within the school.

(Morris *et al.* 1995: 92)

Except for the statutory provision of careers services analysed in some detail in this chapter very little is known about the services offered in the private sector. There are of course, careers counsellors employed by most reputable institutions of higher education. Some further education colleges too have their own guidance counsellors. How many of these persons are actually qualified to offer personal counselling in addition to traditional careers guidance is unknown. However, outside academia, there are a few fairly well-known providers of careers guidance and counselling, who advertise regularly in the national press. An Institute of Personnel and Development (IPD) directory lists about 130 consultancies, most of which are described as small businesses or sole operators working on a self-employed basis. Some of these agencies provide large companies with outplacement and redundancy counselling, helping to prepare employees with their resumes, and giving advice on interview techniques and presentational skills.

The CIPD Code of Conduct Directory of Career and Outplacement Consultants (1995, cited in Riddick *et al.* 1997) defines career and outplacement consultants as

people who provide counselling and services to enable individuals to develop a greater awareness of their capacities, skills
and limitations, to identify and pursue the career opportunities
open to them and to manage the transition through a career
change or into re-employment following a job loss.

(quoted in Riddick *et al.* 1996: 13)

Although there is a lack of any systematic information to draw
conclusions, it is possible that among such consultants, who charge
substantial fees from clients who can afford their services, true, or
generic careers counsellors may be found.

COMPETENCIES

The following is a list that, although not in any way comprehensive or authoritative, may be seen as minimal competencies for the
practice of careers counselling. A careers counsellor:

1 knows the developmental stages of a helping relationship;
2 is familiar with common reactions to a helping relationship (e.g.
   defence mechanisms, transference, modelling and identification,
   culturally related responses, verbal and non-verbal responses);
3 possesses good oral and interpersonal communication skills;
4 writes clearly and grammatically and can prepare reports, letters
   and resumes;
5 can listen and communicate empathy, unconditional positive
   regard, genuineness, and acceptance;
6 can effectively conduct an interview or discussion with people from
   various educational, cultural, and socioeconomic backgrounds;
7 is familiar with the appropriate use, interpretation, strengths,
   and limitations of instruments that are widely used in assessing
   aptitudes, intelligence, abilities, interests, values, and personality;
8 understands the changing patterns and meaning of work in
   modern society;
9 understands the lifelong process of career development and the
   broad scope of career counselling;
10 is familiar with careers information and knows how to help
   people acquire and use this information;
11 can promote improved life/work planning via client self-exploration, values clarification, development of alternatives, decision
   making, reality testing and leisure counselling;
12 can help people develop the skills needed for effective job seeking (e.g. interview skills, c.v. writing);

13 is aware of and appreciates individual, lifestyle, and cultural differences;
14 can take account of the effect that a varied cultural and environmental background can have on a person's development;
15 can help people who represent special populations to become aware of their needs and set their own priorities and goals, and can accept the validity of their wants.

How this works in practice and the various historical and contemporary models of counselling that inform counselling activity in careers guidance will be discussed in some depth in the next chapter.

· THREE ·

The practice of counselling in careers guidance

Some indication of the way in which vocational guidance, or careers guidance developed in industrialized countries to meet a diversity of circumstances has been outlined in the two previous chapters. While education and training of the workforce becomes ever more important, educational guidance is no longer limited to school-leavers but has become another strand of adult guidance work. Additionally, in complex, individualistic societies, personal guidance, ranging from advice-giving and group work to individual counselling and psychotherapy, at many career transitional points, has become an almost inevitable third strand of guidance. The increasing popularity of corporate employee assistance programmes attests to this trend (see also Greenwood, forthcoming).

COUNSELLING BY STEALTH

It is probably fair to say that verbal psychotherapies, and more particularly psychoanalysis have had greater acceptance on the other side of the Atlantic than in the United Kingdom. For various historical and cultural reasons behavioural and cognitive behavioural therapies gained a predominant position in the United Kingdom at the expense of psychotherapy (see Davies 1997). This has meant that counselling, a purely verbal intervention, not based on favoured behaviourist theories of learning, did not initially gain ready acceptance in Britain. Even the positions advertised within the schools careers service or at universities are, more often than not, for careers advisers, careers officers or even careers consultants with careers counsellors almost unheard of.

For some time there was probably a popular perception that counselling was a vague activity which smacked of 'tea and sympathy'
that anybody could undertake, and not a serious and purposeful
endeavour based on learned and accredited expertise. There seems
to be a bias in most technological societies towards human activity
that draws upon factual, cognitive, or intellectual resources and is
portrayed as 'scientific', against occupations that could be termed
'artistic', or simply regarded as 'an art', which could not be subjected
to analysis and systematization. Emotions, in such a context, are seen
as inconvenient, getting in the way of the objective, impartial and
logical application of knowledge. Human sciences like experimental
psychology having deliberately taken a positivistic, deterministic
stance, extensively researched concepts like 'intelligence', but had
very little to say about emotions, which are not readily amenable
to 'operational' definitions and testing in laboratories. Hence their
neglect, even when emotions are palpably important in so much of
what happens, for example, in career choice and decision making.

Compounding the issue, with Freud, Jung, Adler and the early
psychotherapists falling out among themselves, there has been a
plethora of warring factions, with theorizing hardly based on any
agreement even on the fundamentals of psychotherapy as a discipline. It has been difficult to shake off the associations with medicine, psychiatry and 'head shrinking'. Nevertheless, as has been
repeated in the literature, counselling in its modern form owes its
existence to the American psychologist Carl Rogers, with the word
'counselling' consciously chosen, to rid the activity of negative associations historically attached to psychotherapy. Also, many of the
key concepts in counselling have been 'operationalized' and to a
great extent independently and consensually validated.

Although Carl Rogers's non-directive, client-centred counselling
caught on in the United States in the early 1950s, it took two
decades or more for it to take even a limited hold in the United
Kingdom. The Standing Conference for the Advancement of Counselling was established in 1971, while the first issue of the *British
Journal of Guidance and Counselling* appeared in 1973. However, it
still took some time for counselling to be recognized as useful in
'careers advisory work' since in the United Kingdom, counselling
was initially restricted to educational and personal counselling. However, 'by 1973, a counselling element was introduced to the basic
courses for training careers officers . . . "Guidance and Counselling"
had become one of the key areas to be assessed in the diploma' [in
careers guidance] (Holdsworth 1982: 88). As Ruth Holdsworth maintains, 'concepts and practice of counselling {was [*sic*] introduced} to

careers advisers in higher education, . . . *under the less worrying title of interview training'* (1982: 88, my italics). This shows the extent to which there was antipathy in careers guidance to the very idea of counselling at the time.

Ruth Holdsworth (1982: 88) continues:

In 1975 the National Institute for Career Education and Counselling (NICEC) was established, a combined venture of Hatfield Polytechnic and the Careers Research and Advisory Centre (CRAC), and this again has been a major contributor to the development of careers counselling within educational establishments *under the cover, in its early courses, of the title 'Interviewing Relationships and Skills'*.

(my italics)

It took two more years for the British Association for Counselling (BAC) to come into existence and a further year (1978) before the Counselling at Work Division of the BAC was established. Surprisingly, it then suddenly became a fad or a shibboleth for management who jumped on the bandwagon with 'appraisal counselling, career development counselling, redundancy counselling and pre-retirement counselling' (Holdsworth 1982: 88).

Mention has been made of the fact that counselling has sometimes had to be introduced through the back door, as it were . . . on the one hand, the few evangelists (some dangerously near to seeing counselling as the panacea of all ills [*sic*]); on the other the die-hards who, if they used the word counselling at all, saw it as applicable to pathological cases only; and in the middle, the bulk of careers advisers presenting an ambivalent front (if it is possible to do this), feeling their way forward until they could see how the new ideas and techniques could be incorporated in their work.

(Holdsworth 1982: 89)

Barrie Hopson, an influential figure in the counselling movement in Britain contributed the chapter on 'Counselling and Helping' to Holdsworth's *Psychology of Careers* (1982). He asserts that 'counselling is only one form of helping' (1982: 93), and lists six different types of helping strategies of which 'counselling' is the last on the list. They are: giving advice; giving information; direct action; teaching; systems change; and counselling' (1982: 94). In placing the activities subsumed under counselling in context, Hopson attempts to demystify the concept, which had, as we saw, such contrasting, and emotionally charged effects on individuals engaged in careers work.

Strangely enough, in the United States one of the earliest books written at a time when helping youngsters into appropriate careers was called vocational guidance, was the book by E.G. Williamson, *How to Counsel Students: A Manual of Techniques for Clinical Counsellors* (1939). This was a six-step 'directive counselling' process rather different from Carl Rogers's later method of non-directive, client-centred counselling. The six steps consisted of analysis; synthesis; diagnosis; prognosis; counselling; and follow-up.

For Williamson, *diagnosis* was the sorting out of relevant from irrelevant facts by a process of logical reasoning eliciting a consistent pattern to the client's career concerns. *Analysis* meant collecting information by using both objective and subjective techniques on attitudes, interests, family background, knowledge, education etc. *Synthesis* was summarizing data by means of case-study techniques to highlight a client's uniqueness and individuality. *Diagnosis* was describing the characteristics of the problem that the client faced by comparing their profile with occupational or educational profiles available. *Prognosis* was judging the probable consequences of the client's problem and indicating alternatives and adjustments that were needed to be made to reach a declared goal. *Counselling* (and this was also called 'treatment') was 'cooperatively' advising the client in conveying a course of action to follow and making adjustments to reach the desired goal. *Follow-up* meant the repetition of the above steps as new problems arose, giving further assistance to the client as and when needed.

This is obviously somewhat different from what is generally regarded as counselling today, but hardly any different to how most careers advisers and careers officers work with their university students, secondary school pupils and other similar client groups in Britain (Stoney *et al.* 1998). As late as 1963, Frank L. Sievers could distinguish between guidance and counselling as follows: 'The two words are not synonymous. Guidance, the bigger term, includes counselling as one of its 6 elements' (quoted in Hopson and Hayes 1968: 279). Sievers's six elements, reminiscent of Williamson's six steps, are:

1 *Analysis*: Helping the student get facts about himself [*sic*] – from test results, cumulative records, and other means of identifying potentialities and interests.
2 *Information*: Giving him the facts about his environment – about educational and occupational opportunities and requirements.
3 *Orientation*: Helping him to get acquainted with the school program and educational and occupational opportunities and requirements.

4 *Counselling*: Helping him to develop self-understanding and to develop his educational and occupational plans.

5 *Placement*: Helping him carry out those plans.

6 *Follow-up*: Determining how his plans worked out and how effectively the educational programme served him.

With slight variations these steps are even more clearly articulated by Larry Cochran (1997: 40), who drew upon Williamson's work (1939; 1949):

1 Orient a client to career counselling as a rational process of gathering and weighing evidence to make a choice.

2 Gather evidence from diverse sources such as tests, school records, descriptions of achievements and hobbies, family background, parental opinion and so on.

3 From evidence, seek convergence to develop a hypothetical portrait of the client (strengths and weaknesses) and relate that portrait to options.

4 In a clear, deliberate manner, present the portrait to the client and assess prospects for success and satisfaction in occupations under consideration.

5 Help the client choose and plan actions to carry out the choice.

6 Schedule a follow-up interview in which progress can be assessed and difficulties of implementation might be resolved.

Cochran (1997: 40–1) agrees that this approach

had great merit, as do recent approaches to build on this . . . First, the steps are easily communicated to clients, providing a clear basis for cooperation. Second, the steps can be easily learned; they are clear, concise and related to a convincing progression . . . the logic of the steps is evident. Third, [it] provides a frame of reference to know where one stands in the process. Even if counsellor and client pause (for whatever reason), the steps provide the framework for getting back on the main track.

However, Cochran sees many disadvantages as well as advantages in the six-step programme and advocates a narrative approach, where in a more flexible, idiographic, and updated version, he turns the steps, or 'units of career counselling', into 'episodes'. A novel approach developed in the United States but little known in the United Kingdom, it is discussed and included among the six main theories of careers counselling later in this chapter.

In Britain, careers work is still performed within the framework of a skills developing and matching or directing-into-the-right slot

approach, as is underscored by a speech made by the then Employment Secretary Mrs Gillian Shephard at the first Conference of
Careers Service Chairmen and Chief Executives on the occasion of
the Careers Service being divested from local authority and central-
ized state control (Shephard 1996).

> Young people need education, training and guidance. It is also
> important that young people's choices are guided in the right
> direction to meet the needs of employers. Too many lose their
> way. They waste their time; time that cannot be replaced.
> They cannot afford to do that. Nor can we allow them to. The
> Careers Service, therefore, has a vital role to play in:
> - providing information on all the available options and on
>   changes in the labour market;
> - giving the appropriate help that young people need to secure
>   the next step in education, training or employment;
> - planning and delivering careers education and guidance jointly
>   with schools and colleges;
> - being flexible enough to respond to local needs and work in
>   partnership with other players locally.

The rationale for bringing together education and employment
under one government department, according to the Minister, was
to enable the Careers Service 'to bridge the gap between education
and employment'. She exhorted careers advisers to 'spend . . . time
with employers . . . understand their needs, understand the trends
in each industry, learn the needs of the labour market, so that
labour market realism can inform their guidance work'.

THE GUIDANCE INTERVIEW

Enough has been said for it to become evident, as Crites (1981)
asserted, that careers guidance/counselling has been and still is a
pragmatic enterprise rather than a theory-driven professional practice. For instance, the six-step programme of the early careers counsellors is essentially a three-stage contract between the counsellor
and client. A diagnosis of the client's career problems is made at the
beginning. In the middle stage comes the process of intervention
using any theories, models or heuristics that the counsellor has at
their command. At the ending stage the outcomes are reviewed and
evaluated. Far too often, careers officers and advisers have been
compelled to cram all three stages into one or two interviews lasting from 45 minutes to an hour at the most. Indeed, as far back as

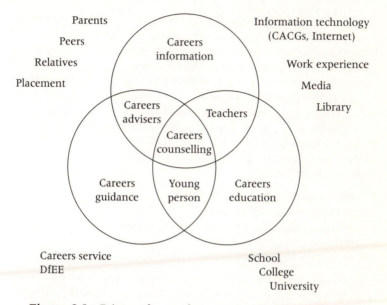

Parents
Peers
Relatives
Placement

Careers information

Information technology
(CACGs, Internet)
Work experience
Media
Library

Careers advisers

Teachers

Careers counselling

Careers guidance

Young person

Careers education

Careers service
DfEE

School
College
University

Figure 3.1 Primary locus of careers counselling in the UK

1987, a senior careers counsellor at a polytechnic wrote, 'careers services have progressively abandoned a client-centred approach founded solely on individual counselling in favour of a continuous guidance programme of seminars, and group guidance services on the grounds of greater cost-effectiveness' (Ball 1987: 6). It is necessary to contrast the above with a statement made almost a decade later in a letter written by another former senior careers adviser turned independent consultant. However, it may be more a statement of intention than a reflection of the actuality, even though it appears to point at the ever-expanding context of careers guidance and counselling (see Figure 3.1).

> Guidance should properly be viewed as an ongoing, longitudinal process, informed by significant others such as family, friends, the media and the school (including but not confined to the formal inputs of a careers education programme) which is sometimes, and perhaps in an ideal world would always be, focused through a quality interaction or series of interactions with a skilled careers adviser. The interview at best thus serves as a focal point for the developmental careers guidance process. It in no way defines the entirety of that process.
>
> (Evans 1996: 30)

As Ruth Holdsworth suggests, long before counselling in its present form came on the scene, the one-to-one guidance interview had been the ubiquitous instrument through which career advice was imparted to the young who did not, or were not able, to benefit from other interventions such as class presentations or group work. Advice rather than counselling was the preferred mode, where this was probably only one stage removed from talks or formal presentations to a group of pupils. Again, common sense and pragmatics provided the basis for the methods advocated. For example, Williamson (1949) recommended the following sequence under interview techniques:

1 establishing rapport,
2 cultivating self-understanding,
3 advising in planning a programme of action,
4 carrying out the plan, and,
5 referral to additional assistance (where need is identified).

It is clear from the above list that more than one interview, usually at least three, over a relatively short but extended period of time, was envisaged. However, in the United Kingdom, resource constraints have traditionally limited the guidance interview to just one session with a careers adviser or careers officer, if at all.

Psychometric test interpretation and occupational information provision, which were incorporated into vocational guidance (as it was called then), showed the influence of early trait-factor theories of occupational matching and choice. While tests uncovered a client's aptitude, potential, skills, strengths and weaknesses, occupational information uncovered the structure of the world of work, employment opportunities, trends and forecasts.

The rationale for psychometric testing as explained by Alec Rodger (1952) was that 'every occupation has an optimum requirement in terms of the aptitudes, abilities, personality characteristics and interests of the workers involved in it' and that testing was an economical and valid means of finding out about these characteristics. However, in many instances comparisons were based on empirically devised profiles of successful incumbents in jobs and not derived from any convincingly articulated theory. The Strong Vocational Interest Blank (Strong 1943), one of the first of its kind, which was influential at the time, continues to be used widely, revised and improved over the years in response to growing theoretical sophistication.

The implied meta-theory or tacit assumption is that jobs are best done by people who are most fitted to do them, and that people are most happy when they exercise their abilities, skills and interests, and that this is a desirable state of affairs. In spite of this, the World Health Organization (WHO) reported in 1992 that one half of the entire working population were unhappy in their jobs and as many as 90 per cent may be spending much of their time and energy in work that brings them no closer to their goals in life. More alarmingly, the WHO reported that about 75 per cent of those who consulted psychiatrists were experiencing problems that could be traced to a lack of job satisfaction.

CAREER THEORY

From about the middle of the twentieth century, academics in vocational and counselling psychology took up the task of theory building in vocational guidance, now referred to as career guidance in the United States and careers (plural) guidance in Britain. These theories, more or less influential, reflect the varying, and often seemingly irreconcilable, traditions in academic psychology. Practically all of them appear to have originated in the United States, with contributions from British theorists and academics who continue to elaborate and revise them to suit local conditions. The six major theories influential in the practice of careers counselling are discussed briefly below.

Patricia Lunneborg (1983) in outlining the major theories under 'Career Counselling Techniques' included 'systematic counselling' and 'non-traditional career counselling', which have not been thought of as meriting separate treatment here as major approaches in Table 3.1. Nor have 'social psychological' or 'computer assisted' theories as summarized by Bruce Walsh (1990) been thought to require inclusion, as these increasingly tend to be incorporated into counselling within other theories.

What has been a notable new addition is constructionist (or constructivist) theory, listed under the narrative approach, as an exciting new development in careers counselling. Other terms used to describe this approach, at least in the exploratory, initial stages, were 'hermeneutic' and 'contextual'.

In her attempt at identification and labelling the various approaches, Patricia Lunneborg (in Walsh and Osipow 1983) requested information on the theoretical orientations of graduate 'counsellor education programs' of the respondent universities, but no psychology department claimed to adhere to any one model or approach. She was fobbed off with comments that they now

'teach schemes which help practitioners know when to apply a
wide variety of techniques,' and that they 'teach trainees how
career developments interact with life adjustment in general,'
and that 'the hallmark [of outstanding graduate counselling
programs] is not in techniques as much as it is in a graduate
training program involving psychology, education, and counselling to produce a steady stream of functioning professionals.'

(Lunneborg 1983: 42)

It appears that when asked directly nobody was willing to nail
their colours to the mast of any particular theory or approach to
careers counselling.

For quite some time the need to reconcile theory with practice
had been perceived to be so acute that in May 1994 a conference
was convened under the rubric 'Toward the Convergence of Career
Theory and Practice' by the Vocational Special Interest Group of the
American Psychological Association. A number of eminent theorists
from the United States, Canada and Britain participated. The proceedings were published in 1996 edited by Mark Savickas and Bruce
Walsh entitled *Handbook of Career Counseling Theory and Practice*. In
their introduction the editors declare:

A series of studies has confirmed the belief that theory is little
used by practitioners . . . Practitioners need knowledge of how
to produce beneficial results in clients. They get it from experience with clients, oral tradition, and emerging research about
the process of psychotherapy, not from [careers] theory and
research.

(Savickas and Walsh 1996: xi)

Practically all the theoretical approaches summarized in this chapter
were revisited at the conference by spokespersons eager to show
how theory and practice were linked for each of the theories. Samuel
Osipow, a distinguished theorist in the field of career guidance
ends his contribution under 'Closing Comments' with the following
impassioned plea:

the point I would like to make most strongly comes in the form
of an admonishment to both theorist/researchers and practitioners. To those practitioners who think that theory doesn't
inform you in your practice, I have some advice. Be less passive
about applying theory. Don't wait for theorists to do all the
work for you. You are smart enough to extrapolate from theory
to practical applications. In addition, in order for the academi-
cians among us to do relevant research and develop cogent

theories, you need to let us study what you do, how you do it, with whom you do your work, and the outcomes you experience. How can we study counseling if we don't have access to the process and procedures? How can we develop connections between career theory and practice without the help of our colleagues in practice? Please collaborate with us.

(Savickas and Walsh 1996: 408)

The six major theories outlined here are broadly distinguishable, and are so dealt with in the literature, although in practice they appear to shade into each other, as practising careers guidance advisers and counsellors tend to be more or less eclectic with little regard to the boundaries erected by pioneering academics and theorists in psychology. This is seen as a better approach than when practitioners doggedly follow the 'one best way' to the detriment of their clients.

In Table 3.1, the six theories, or approaches, are summarized under seven headings for ease of comparison. For example, under the first heading of 'epistemology' the trait-factor approach is labelled deterministic/pragmatic while the narrative approach is labelled hermeneutic/constructionist. To what extent any particular approach has been influential in the past is indicated in the second row. The third heading is an estimation of the potential of the approach for the future. The fourth is about the possibility of the various approaches converging and the extent of that convergence. The fifth heading is about whether or not, or to what extent psychometric tests are used in any particular approach to counselling in career guidance. The sixth deals with typical interview or counselling techniques used in each of the approaches. The last and seventh heading sketches in the characteristics of client group or groups that are most likely to benefit from each approach.

The *trait-factor*, which later evolved into the person-environment fit theory, is the oldest theory underpinning the practice of vocational guidance and careers counselling. This approach, derived from modern scientific psychology at the turn of the twentieth century still has powerful and loyal adherents. E.G. Williamson (1939; 1949) based his work entirely on this Parsonian model. It was the pioneering activity of matching people to jobs, which has also been referred to as the differentialist approach. Invariably a battery of tests is administered to the client. Test results are normative and held to be stable over time, which emphasizes actuarial methods. The instruments used are demonstrated to be reliable and valid. Differential diagnosis is a prerequisite of this problem solving, cognitive

Table 3.1 Six main approaches to counselling in careers guidance

	Trait-Factor	Developmental	Psychodynamic	Client-centred	Social learning	Narrative
Epistemology	Deterministic/ Pragmatic	Pragmatic/ Deterministic	Deterministic/ Hermeneutic	Humanistic	Deterministic	Hermeneutic/ Constructionist
Past Influence	Extensive	Extensive	Limited	Pervasive	Extensive	Minimal
Potential	Continuing	Expanding	Specialized	Ubiquitous	Selective	Unknown
Convergence	Possible	Possible	Unlikely	Probable	Selectively	Unlikely
Test Usage	Bedrock Actuarial	Optional	Limited Projective	Optional	Limited	Rarely used
Interview Techniques	Feedback Interpret interests, values, personality, aptitudes and potential	Inductive/ deductive reasoning to discover new cognitive and affective associations	Explore life themes choosing vocations that are socially viable and personally suitable	Relate with empathy, genuineness and unconditional positive regard. Locus of control with client	Reinforcement of desirable responses. Social modelling. Impart decision making skills	Joint meaningful construction of life-span, life-space narrative as basis for action
Appropriate Client Group	Most groups, especially new entrants to world of work	Most groups, probably less effective with marginal groups	Vocationally uncommitted, indecisive clients. Some marginal groups	Most groups, specifically articulate and autonomous clients	Most groups, especially those presenting career problems and career changers	Most groups, clients in career transition and most marginal groups

approach. The goal of counselling is to give valid and objective information to the client both of themselves and about the world of work so that the client gains cognitive mastery of the careers domain both in the present and for the future. Goal setting and action planning are also important aspects of this model.

An eminent defender of this approach is John Holland who developed a typology of personality characteristics with matching patterns of preferences for occupations. The six occupational types are labelled: Realistic, Investigative, Artistic, Social, Enterprising and Conventional. This is a hexagonal model with the six occupational types placed at the vertices in the RIASEC order clockwise. The model has been intensively researched with moderate support for some occupational types showing significant presence in predicted environments as against others. Counsellors, or more correctly advisers, usually adopt an authoritative, assertive stance. Increasingly the instruments of assessment are computerized and readily available for self-administration. A weakness of this model is the assumption that the characteristics measured, whether of personality or environment, are more or less invariant over time. However, recent apologists for this approach appear to be aware of the need for, and the capacity for, change in their clients. They are also much less directive due to the major paradigm shift in counselling following Carl Rogers's work (Swanson 1996: 93–108).

Crites (1981) criticized this approach and claimed that it had been often caricatured as 'three interviews and a cloud of dust', the 'cloud of dust' indicating that the client was often left to his or her own devices after the usual 'test and tell' session. A more recent critic has been Krumboltz, the originator of the 'social learning' approach, who claimed that it 'oversimplifies the complexities of helping people with a wide range of career problems' (1993: 15). However, Swanson argued that 'over the years, applications of trait-and-factor counseling have responded to the needs of clients, yet these changes have not always been incorporated back into the theoretical statements' (1996: 104).

In spite of 30 or more years of criticism, careers counselling along trait-factor lines continue due mainly to its simplicity, economy, and ease of use.

Developmental theorists, of whom Donald Super is the exemplar, espoused a clinical approach where Super (1957) introduces the self-concept as central to career decision making. He uses the idea of the self-concept as the locus of vocational choice and development throughout one's life span. The role of the counsellor is to assist the client to clarify and implement a worthwhile, reality-based vocational self-concept. Based on the work of Charlotte Buehler (1933) and Erik Erikson (1963), the pioneering developmental psychologists who espoused stage theories of human development, Super postulates five stages of development of the vocational self-concept over the life span. These are growth (age 0–14), exploration (age 15–24), establishment (25–44), maintenance (45–64), and decline (age 65 onwards). However, outside the middle-class, white, male, Anglo-Saxon population sample of his early research, it has been pointed out that such a neat chronology is unlikely to be relevant to a sizeable proportion of today's workers. Super has extended the concept of career to include nine separate major roles, which may be appropriate to different life stages, the role of worker being only one of them. The nine roles are child, student, 'leisureite', citizen, worker, spouse, homemaker, parent and pensioner. These roles are played out in four 'theatres' – home, school, community, and the workplace. For the developmentalist, a career is the combination and sequence of many roles played by a person during his or her lifetime.

Developmentalist assumptions about careers are listed in abbreviated form by Jepsen (Savickas and Walsh 1996: 135–6):

(a) development is a self-constructive process;
(b) a person's activity has both structure and function;
(c) a person functions as a unified system; and
(d) new subsystems of action emerge from old subsystems of action but in different forms.

Donald Super is credited with introducing the idea of 'career' as against the then prevailing 'vocational' or 'occupational' model of guidance. He proposes varying strategies for careers education at different stages of the life cycle. He has been also instrumental in moving the locus of concern from society, or the economy, to the individual, with his notion of developing and implementing the 'self-concept'. He shows that job roles are reciprocally related to social roles in his model of the 'life-career rainbow'.

Super (1957) has described his theory, which he has kept building over the years, as segmental. Although it is meant to be comprehensive, some parts of it are more relevant to some clients at a particular time or stage in their lives.

The *psychodynamic* approach to careers counselling with Ann Roe (1956) as a pioneering theorist was later developed by E.S. Bordin (1955) and others. Psychodynamic theorists hold work to be a means of sublimation of instinctual drives. They interpret vocational problems in terms of wishes and defences. The goal is to reduce neurotic conflict in career decision making and progression, resulting in positive personality change. In effect, neurotic symptoms are turned into strengths, which in turn are converted into socially useful contributions as jobs in the working world. Psychodynamic counsellors use structured interviews, projective techniques, autobiographies and card sorts eliciting intra-individual, or idiographic characteristics, very different from the trait-factor theorists' nomothetic, actuarial use of test data. Clients are helped to identify and develop life themes 'making intelligible interconnections among the episodes of the client's life' (Walsh and Osipow 1990: 272).

Watkins and Savickas (1990) identify four types of clients who appear to benefit most from the psychodynamic approach to careers counselling describing them as 1) indecisive and unrealistic clients, 2) difficult clients, 3) mid-career changers, and 4) displaced home-makers (in the United Kingdom, probably those referred to as women returners). Tainted by accusations of being a pseudo-science the psychodynamic model applied to careers counselling may not be described as a favoured mainstream approach, although it appears to fill in the gaps left by those who are ill-served by a totally rational, cognitive, or behavioural orthodoxy.

As Richard Nelson-Jones (1982: 152) when critiquing Super's developmental theory observed:

> the process of occupational choice involves not just an external compromise between the individual and the world of work, but also some form of compromise between the individual's own needs and residues of parental and cultural influences. The notion of autonomy in Super's recent work goes some, but not all, of the way towards evaluating the extent to which people are open to their *own* experience and, also, do not have their decision-making distorted by anxiety and unexamined internalizations of other people's values.

Where the rational process of career decision-making is contaminated with debilitating neurotic concerns, psychodynamic counselling promises to unloosen the grip on the individual of the irrational, whether this is described as unconscious forces, drives, instincts, conditioning, instrumental learning or any other internalized influence outside the clients' cognitive awareness.

The *client-centred*, or the person-centred approach, derives very much from Carl Rogers's original work in the field of psychotherapy. The aim is to create an accepting, safe, psychological climate where the client can explore and develop a personal, worthwhile work identity by establishing a clear and satisfying vocational goal. The counsellor relates to the client with empathy, genuineness, respect, and unconditional positive regard. The locus of control is with the client at all times. No testing is undertaken, unless the clients expressly wish to subject themselves to a testing procedure with material selected by collaborative agreement. Counsellors are expected to disclose results in a non-evaluative, non-judgemental manner.

The process of client-centred career counselling is the here-and-now, person-to-person interaction which promotes self-discovery in the client. Although there is no 'treatment planning' the counsellor is however, unlike in therapy, expected to have knowledge and skills in gathering and presenting relevant career information for clients' use. Clients are also free to seek their own information and interpret it in unique ways without the intervention of the counsellor.

This approach is easily generalizable across most of the other career counselling approaches, and as seen earlier, has been adopted by most of them consciously as a valid technique, although the commitment and competence of individual practitioners may vary widely in practice.

In contrast to the client-centred approach, the *social learning* approach or learning theory of careers counselling is very much a counsellor-centred intervention. The counsellor reinforces verbally and behaviourally any activity on the part of clients that might advance them strategically towards a clearly formulated career goal. John Krumboltz is a leading proponent of the cognitive behavioural approach to careers counselling. In addition to reinforcement, the counsellor uses modelling techniques to guide clients towards relevant information seeking and exploratory behaviour directly influencing changes in what Krumboltz terms *self-observation generalizations* of the client.

Krumboltz (1996) postulates four influencers of career decision making. They are:

1 genetic endowments and special abilities (e.g. race, sex, predispositions, talents);
2 environmental conditions and events (e.g. educational and job opportunities, resources, legal constraints and technology);
3 learning experiences (e.g. instrumental learning, classical conditioning, modelling);
4 task approach skills (e.g. perceptual and cognitive processes, work habits, mental sets, emotional responses).

Since occupational matching is no longer seen as the sine qua non of careers counselling, Krumboltz lists some even more important concerns for any career theory. These include locus of control, career

obstacles, job search knowledge, job search motivation, job relationships, job burnout, occupational advancement, and retirement planning, which are all addressed by the social learning theory approach.

Richard Nelson-Jones (1982: 159) summarizes the process of counselling in social learning theory as follows:

> The processes of career selection are complex, since they rep-
> resent the intersection of many influences over a long period
> of time. The role of the careers counsellor is to help clients to
> obtain a set of decision-making skills by which career prefer-
> ence, training and entry decisions can be made as rationally as
> possible. Furthermore, counsellors . . . help clients both to set
> up appropriate career-exploration learning experiences and to
> evaluate the personal consequences of these experiences.

The social learning theory of careers guidance is a relatively new
approach based on the self-efficacy concept developed by Albert
Bandura in his pioneering research into learning theory. Since the
emphasis is on altering behaviour, assessments using psychometric
instruments are rare. Nevertheless, Krumboltz has developed the
Career Beliefs Inventory used to identify self-limiting beliefs that act
as barriers to career goal achievement.

The *narrative* approach is a practice-based theory developed in
the 1990s, which is of and for the postindustrial, postmodern
society, although its roots can be traced to William James, the great
nineteenth-century American psychologist. Mark Savickas (in Cochran
1997: vi) writes that almost all methods of vocational guidance
in the past relied too heavily on 'scientific techniques devised by
applied psychologists, [overemphasizing] the objective dimension
of career development. Although traits provide a convincing basis for
actuarial predictions, they do not comprehend human purpose and
passion'. As early as 1986, British and Canadian academics had been
urging that a career theory ought to be 'ecological, biographical,
and hermeneutical' (Collin and Young 1992: 1).

Collin and Young (1992: 1–2) argued that:

> there is a changing framework for the understanding of social
> realities such as career that strengthens our call for new direc-
> tions in theory and causes us to recognize the evolving mean-
> ing that is attributed both individually and socially to constructs
> such as vocation and career. Our argument for the interpretive
> or hermeneutical study of career draws on an approach that is
> premised on the historically and socially constructed nature of
> social meaning.

While not rejecting the contribution made by aptitude tests, interest inventories and occupational information, Larry Cochran in the preface to his book *Career Counselling, A Narrative Approach* (1997: viii) points out that: 'Suitable employment is not only about matching, but also about the proper vehicle through which a certain character can be enacted in a certain kind of drama'. Cochran introduces the concept of 'emplotment' to replace matching, 'that is, how a person can be cast as the main character in a career narrative that is meaningful, productive and fulfilling' (1997: ix). His aim is to introduce those counsellors who have 'been dissatisfied with the limits of the objective tradition' to a 'subjective approach to career counselling that emphasizes meaning and meaning-making while retaining the merits of the traditional, objective approach' (1997: ix). His conclusion is that the 'task of career counselling is to help people construct and enact more meaningful career narratives' (1997: x).

In contrast to the trait-factor approach, which is static in terms of the steps that the counsellor imposes, the narrative approach elicits the reality of a continuous process of future representation moving from relative 'disorder to order, from exploration to crystallization in which meanings are stabilised' (Cochran 1997: 14).

The notion of career, according to this model, is subjective and 'self-invested' and its representations tend to be 'rhetorical or dramatic, intended to move as well as to persuade or convince' through literary 'devices such as metaphor, analogy, model, hyperbole, synecdoche, and irony' (Cochran 1997: 2).

Collin and Young (1992: 2) contrast the premises of other theories with the narrative approach while underscoring their position:

> Our thesis is that, in order to make sense of the events of their world, people have to interpret those events in terms that are meaningful to them. Academics may legitimately construe such events as technological change, manifestation of career readiness, or person–environment fit, but individuals make sense of the raw material by 'storying' experience through metaphor and narrative. Such a story makes sense of the life as it is led by putting life events in perspective. Thus in order both to study career and counsel others about their careers, we have to interpret the words and stories people use to construct their careers.

To make sense of one's life, within the context of what one does for a living, a coherent narrative has to be constructed, which is mediated through language, reflecting history, culture, society, relationships and much else. Career, as 'an important modern project' is the framework through which people tell stories about themselves.

Counsellors 'interpret' these stories collaboratively through shared meanings to 'develop ever more suitable frames for their experience' (Young and Collin 1992: 11).

In this postmodern approach to careers counselling and guidance, the self-concept, which is at the very heart of developmental theory, is questioned and the functional analysis of more or less stable clusters of skills, strengths, interests and values as the 'traditional cornerstone of career theory' becomes problematic. 'To the extent that these interpretations are based on generalizations from research findings, theoretical models, or other universal axioms or assumptions, they are limited because they cannot account very well for context and meaning' (Young and Collin 1992: 10). From this perspective careers counselling is perceived as no more than an 'administrative science' and even an instrument of 'social control'.

Finally, it must be admitted that counselling in this mode cannot be prescribed. It is more an interpretive stance adopted by the counsellor and a creative moment-by-moment process of joint meaning making. It is easier to point to what it is not. For example:

> The goal of counselling activity is commonly accepted as the autonomy, agency, and empowerment of the client. However, the very constructs imbued in the counsellor through the training process may result in the imposition of meanings that do not derive from the client's own experience; these meanings may stem from the interpretive world of the dominant orthodoxy and may be socially controlling.
>
> (Young and Collin 1992: 12)

Apart from the use of computers to a varying extent in practically all of the above approaches, there is also a technocentric school of thought, which in total opposition to the narrative approach believes that human agency becomes an optional extra, since computers programmed in fuzzy logic can easily simulate the average counsellor. A more realistic view is expressed by Gati (in Savickas and Walsh 1996: 185):

> while CACGSs [computer assisted career guidance systems] can replace some of the counsellors' traditional roles (e.g. assessing vocational interests, eliciting preferences, identifying promising alternatives, and providing information), they also allow them to devote more time to their other roles as counsellors. These other roles include providing refined judgments and sensitive evaluations, as in identifying preferences that are unrealistic for

the client, dealing with dilemmas that result from conflicting preferences, coping with the influence of significant others, restructuring the decision, reframing the compromises involved to reduce their negative consequences . . . and exploring ways to increase the prospects of realizing an attractive alternative.

Some of the computer programs developed in the United Kingdom and used extensively are CASCAID, JIIG-CAL, Microdoors and Adult Directions. In addition almost all test publishers have computer testing and reporting facilities which are of course available to test users accredited by the British Psychological Society. There are increasingly a number of websites on the Internet, which not only include testing but also dispense careers guidance.

Other theories of relatively more limited use but extensively reported in the literature include George Kelly's (1955) Personal Construct Theory of more general application, Linda Gottfredson's (1981) Circumscription and Compromise Theory on how early sex-typing influences later career choices, and Bill Law's (1981) Community Interaction Theory, developed to move the person–environment fit approach towards the person–environment interaction approach. It is also worth mentioning Dawis and Lofquist (1984) with their theory of work adjustment (TWA) dealing with the correspondence between personal needs and job reinforcers, and between personal abilities and job requirements.

Lunneborg (1983) has reproduced, based on others' work, a dimensional framework for careers counselling which when applied to the theories listed above, shows a tendency over a period of time to move from left to right. However it would be a mistake to think that the movement indicates progress in every situation. Counsellors must have at their command the entire repertoire so that they can utilize the whole range of the dimensions in furthering any individual client's unique career and personal goals.

The dimensions may not be exhaustive, but adapted from Lunneborg (1983: 43), they are mainly:

1 specific outcome versus nonspecific outcome;
2 content emphasis versus process emphasis;
3 point-in-time decision versus developmental/longitudinal goal;
4 didactic format versus experiential format;
5 other-selected participation versus self-selected participation;
6 increased information goal versus increased internality goal;
7 passive counsellee versus active counsellee;
8 passive counsellor versus active counsellor;
9 counselling as treatment versus stimulus;

10 present oriented versus future oriented;
11 cognitive emphasis versus affective emphasis;
12 ameliorative versus preventive effort.

CAREER COUNSELLING COMPETENCIES

Before concluding this chapter it is necessary to look at the competencies required for the practice of careers counselling in Britain today. A NICEC/CRAC Briefing Paper, *Staff Development for Careers Work in Schools and Sixth-Form Colleges* (1995) outlining current provision for the development of teachers and lecturers might be adopted as a specification of the generic competencies needed for effective careers guidance and counselling.

Under the heading 'Starting Points', the briefing paper stresses knowledge of the world of work, education and training, and careers theory. Next comes organizing and using careers information and computers within a resource centre. Under 'Guidance and Support' it mentions only individual guidance skills, although omission of interview skills could be an oversight. Under 'Reporting, Recording and Reviewing' are listed records of achievement (RoA) and action plans. Under 'Classroom Work' are listed developing careers education programmes, teaching careers education and preparing material. Under 'Cross-Curricular Work' comes managing and coordinating careers work programmes and informing, supporting and training other teachers. Work experience and other community links, including liaising with parents, are listed under 'Community-linked Work'. Finally, under 'Managing Careers Work', liaison with the Careers Service, updating policy and practice with evaluating and influencing, are mentioned.

A Career Theories printout from an Education User Website (24/7/98) gives the following as 'Career Counseling Competencies', revealing another useful perspective on the range of knowledge, skills and attitudes involved:

- career development theory – theories and associated techniques, theories and models, differences related to gender, race ... human development across the life span;
- individual and group counseling skills – personal/professional relationships, collaboration, techniques, personal characteristics involved, social contextual influences, development, decision making, attitudes;

- individual and group assessment – aptitudes, achievement, interests, values, personality, leisure activities, work environment, computer-delivered methods;
- information resources – education, training and employment trends, resources, roles of men and women;
- program promotion, management and implementation – designs that can be used, needs assessments, budgeting, planning, leadership roles;
- coaching, consulting and performance improvement – consultation strategies and relationships;
- diverse populations – multicultural counseling competencies;
- supervision – recognize limitations, supervise others, consult with supervisors;
- ethical/legal issues;
- research/evaluation;
- computer competencies.

An independent survey published by the Department for Education and Employment in November 1998 was 'a small, but intensive study' on 'young people's reaction to careers education and guidance (CEG)' (Stoney *et al.* 1998: 7). The picture that emerges is less sanguine. Chapter 3 is headed 'What Young People Do Not Want'. The pupils' criticisms of what they received from careers advisers fell into three broad categories:

- lack of preparation;
- over-directiveness and inflexibility;
- the need for dialogue.

(Stoney *et al.* 1998: 22)

This is most surprising, when Holdsworth (1982) asserts that all careers advisers are trained in 'guidance and counselling' as part of the diploma, and when a report (Morris *et al.* 1995: 45) produced 'on behalf of the Employment Department Careers Service Branch, Quality Assurance and Development Unit' in June 1995 declares that 'some careers staff were eminently qualified to provide training [to teachers] in one-to-one counselling' (see Chapter 2).

The report on young people's views (Stoney *et al.* 1998) reproduces verbatim a few of their views, which are quite disturbing. The paragraph from which these quotations are taken has the heading 'Directing, advising or counselling?'

> She was . . . not in a nasty way, but . . . she was trying to pressure us into coming back to do the [GNVQ] Advanced, saying that it would be better for me. But it's not what I want to do.

I want to go and get a job. And I felt that, as such, I was being pressurised into coming back to school' . . .

As one [young person] said '[the adviser was] the one who came to the interview without an open mind' . . . 'You say something to the careers [*sic*] and they start saying something else. You say you want to do retail and they say "You are sure you don't want to work in an office?"

(Stoney *et al.* 1998: 22)

The authors' overall conclusion is that:

The careers system appears to be losing young people in all sorts of ways, irrespective of the excellence of individual events and professional inputs that young people could recognise. This is a pity since, with the international emphasis now on lifelong learning, varied career paths and changing working lives, there has never been a greater need for individuals to have the skills, knowledge and attitudes to respond to these changes and chart their way to new opportunities. They need to be open to, and be able to access, professional guidance when they need it at different times of their lives, and early experiences, good or bad, can determine whether they do this effectively in the long term.

(Stoney *et al.* 1998: 46)

Somewhat in contrast to the findings of the above report Peter Lang (1999: 29) writes about 'pupils from some 10 secondary schools' discussing 'their feelings about PSE and their tutors with PGCE students'. Lang, however, is at pains to emphasize that 'the schools had been chosen because there were indications that their approach was at least a developed and thought-through one' (1999: 29). It is clear that in Lang's view what is of crucial importance are the counselling skills and the pupil-centred approach exhibited by teachers responsible for PSE (physical and social education) and pastoral care in schools.

What many pupils liked about PSE was that they could speak their mind and express opinions freely. It was clear that many appreciated the space and voice which they felt it offered them. Equally, there were those who saw it as a waste of time and who felt constrained. Observations on their tutors indicated a full range of relationships. For some, the last person they would talk to was their tutor; for others, the tutor was clearly completely trusted and had offered support that had been appreciated. It was interesting how often the *importance of trust, understanding, approachability and confidentiality* was mentioned.

(Lang 1999: 29, my italics)

These observations of the statuory school careers system define the setting for the hardly visible adult careers guidance and counselling offered in Britain. Since the carreers service has been more or less privatized, fewer and fewer regional services offer careers guidance and counselling to adults simply because they are not required to do so. Some offer these services and charge fees but the take-up is understandably poor. Specific groups identified as disadvantaged in the labour market are increasingly at risk of social exclusion. There are profound changes in the world of work which most analysts see as requiring a better informed, more professional, and inclusive approach to learning, counselling and guidance at the many more transitional points in a person's life-career. These issues will be explored further in the following chapters.

· FOUR ·

Specific issues in counselling in careers guidance

Theoretical developments relating to careers and their choice have been explored in some detail in earlier chapters. Guidance and counselling is the focus of this chapter. 'If career theory aims to explain how people end up in the occupations they do, then guidance theory is about helping those people to manage the stages by which they achieve this – moving from theory to practice' (Fielding, undated: 33). However, for the most part, guidance is practice-based with hardly any formal theory except ad hoc pronouncements and ad hoc models used by practitioners or professionals with training responsibilities. Counselling has a varied but more accessible theory base, which at times distinguishes itself from, and at others identifies with, models of psychotherapy.

GUIDANCE WITHOUT COUNSELLING?

Recent official (e.g. DfEE) and professional (e.g. ICG) documents cited in the last two chapters have been parsimonious in references to counselling in careers guidance. However, practitioners insist that this is a mere matter of terminology and that counselling forms an integral part of their day to day careers work in Britain. They point out that much of the counselling practice and literature originated in the United States, which explains a preference for the ready use of counselling as a generic term over there. Guidance in all its forms is regarded as the more inclusive term in Britain, with counselling seen as one type of process intervention within a guidance context. Guidance is regarded as a helping process broadly in the personal, educational, vocational, health/welfare, family and recreational areas of life. About two million people, over 10 per cent of the United Kingdom workforce, are employed in this service sector. The diversity of this field is reflected in the following quotation:

> Counsellors and psychotherapists work in a range of contexts, including the voluntary sector, health service, youth work, education, social services, prisons, and staff counselling in employment and private practice. There are different theoretical models and practical traditions, which are widely divergent. Definitions of counselling and psychotherapy, and the boundaries between them, are disputed. There are no statutory regulations governing practice in the profession. Accreditation in this field has been developed to suit the requirements of a range of different professional contexts.
>
> (Oakshott 1996: 24)

Guidance work is largely a personal service; therefore moral and ethical principles are expected to inform guidance practice. These superordinate principles or standards are developed, on behalf of the polity and state, by consensus through statutory agencies like the Advice, Guidance, Counselling and Psychotherapy Lead Body. This agency has been recently transmogrified as 'The national organisation for education, training and standards setting in Advice, Advocacy, Counselling, Guidance, Mediation and Psychotherapy' (CAMPAG 1998). Some of the basic principles underpinning guidance practice are listed as:

- accessibility;
- equality of opportunity;
- impartiality;
- confidentiality;
- client autonomy.

Guidance is described as a process of 'clarifying options' and can consist of a selective mix of activities including informing, advising, counselling, assessing, enabling/empowering, advocating and providing feedback. Note that counselling is listed as one of at least seven activities that constitute guidance. However there is a great deal of overlap both conceptually and in practice. Counselling emphasizes the quality of relationship between client and practitioner, whereas guidance at the structural level can be more formal, and in activities such as informing almost impersonal. For example, the use of psychometric tests in the assessment of vocational aptitudes if administered in standard fashion can feel alienating and threatening to some clients. Most agree that in counselling, the interpersonal relationship between client and practitioner is at the heart of the process and must be based on at least three core conditions. These are empathy, warmth and genuineness. The practitioner uses such specific processes as attending (active listening), responding (reflecting back) and understanding (supporting) in a dyadic encounter. The outcome is clarification of and commitment by the client to new tasks and goals or a re-evaluation and an autonomous decision to move from a position of inertia and lack of direction.

THE GUIDANCE INTERVIEW REVISITED

In Britain, traditionally the vocational guidance interview

provided a very particular set of role expectations. The careers specialist, as the acknowledged expert, is expected to provide the correct diagnosis, rather like a general practitioner in medical practice. The interviewee, on the other hand, is likely to be the passive recipient of the prescribed course of action.

(Ball 1984: 48)

More often than not, the careers interview, especially at school or college, was 'a one-off and once for all interview' (Ball 1984: 49). Over the years counselling skills were introduced under the rubric interviewing skills (see Chapter 2), but the recent emphasis on the 'action plan' as an outcome measure as evidence of client commitment has often resulted in an 'uncompromisingly directive' approach.

Early research by Bedford (1982) on 'the process and outcomes of 680 career officer interviews in 200 schools throughout the country' resulted in the finding that 'the factor most closely associated with an effective interview was that of creating a friendly encouraging atmosphere' (Ball 1984: 52). Furthermore,

[T]he interview was not seen as the most appropriate place to try to meet students' information needs. The effectiveness of the interviews was directly dependent on the extent of contact between careers officer and school. Clinic interviews were more effective than 'cold canvassing' [or] blanket interviews.

(Ball 1984: 53)

From such evidence, Ball was able to conclude that the careers interview, for optimal results, must be a helping or counselling interview rather than the traditional diagnostic interview. However, his observation that a counselling interview ought to be 'one of a series of helping encounters' (1984: 49) appears to have made hardly any impact on the school careers interview, which is still almost always a 'one-off'. Increasingly, it is aimed more at the vocationally immature or undecided pupil, while for the vast majority, the matching process is assumed to be more or less unproblematic.

Careers services, most of which are now private companies, 'vary unduly in the amount of time allocated to careers advisers for the conduct of their Year 11 guidance interviews'; as the Ofsted/DfEE *National Survey of Careers Education and Guidance, Secondary Schools* (1998: 21–2) reports on this activity.

> For example, one company expects its careers advisers to complete a Year 11 guidance interview, including the agreement and the production of a careers action plan, in a total of 30 minutes. This is a very demanding task and places a great strain on the careers adviser. In some cases this requirement adversely affects the quality of the guidance interview. Most companies allocate a minimum of 45 minutes to the Year 11 guidance interview and some allow up to one hour. Most companies recognise the importance of allocating more generous time allowances for work with students with special educational needs.

Note the number of times the adjective 'guidance' is used to describe the Year 11 (one-off) interview. There is no reference to helping or counselling as advocated by Ball (1984) which, according to him, should have replaced the diagnostic or information-giving aspects for the interview to become more effective. Allocation of extra time (a measurable outcome) appears to be the sole concern of the authors of the above report. Their recommendations, listed as 'Key issues for action', refer to leadership, management, and partnership agreements, with nothing said about improving the quality of the guidance interview.

There is a glossary in Annex 2 entitled Terminology. Surprisingly, although the word 'counselling' appears here, it is defined in the broadest terms:

> **Counselling** is an integral aspect of guidance. It refers to purposeful relationships, which help individuals to understand and cope more effectively with themselves and their circumstances, and to handle their personal development, their roles and relationships with other people.
>
> (Ofsted/DfEE 1998: 42)

But:

> **Careers guidance** refers to provision through which students are assisted in applying their knowledge, skills and information

to make realistic choices and appropriate decisions about future options. Opportunities are provided for reviewing learning, assessing, setting new goals and recording achievements. Guidance may be provided through interviews and small group work, including action planning and recording of achievement, which help students to implement their personal career plans.

(Ofsted/DfEE 1998: 41)

Counselling appears nowhere in the above explanation of careers guidance, which in the authors' eyes is probably a purely rational and cognitive activity with hardly any impact on the affective domain. The earlier definition of counselling therefore appears to hint at a non-normative pathology on the part of those seeking or requiring counselling, perhaps emphasizing guidance in the context of crises in relationships such as marriage, divorce or bereavement. In a globally volatile job market underlining the need for employability and lifelong learning to stave off the risk of social exclusion of a large proportion of the population, such demarcations appear short-sighted. In spite of official indifference, how individual careers advisers seek to meet a public demand for counselling in adult careers guidance is explored later in the chapter.

First, it would be instructive to see why the authorities fight shy of the concept of counselling in Britain. It is averred that counselling 'arrived in English schools in the 1960s [with] . . . its introduction . . . unco-ordinated and problematic' (Lang 1999: 24). While 'during school counselling's heyday, there were [only about] 350 school counsellors employed in England and Wales' this was reduced to an estimated 90 in 1988. Since then counselling as a school activity has declined even further. Lang asserts that both secondary and primary school teachers' awareness of counselling is of an 'emergency service brought into action after some form of disaster . . . As a result, many teachers' understanding of the nature of counselling is at best very general and at worst mistaken and confused' (1999: 25).

The Education and Reform Act (1988) 'alongside the introduction of the National Curriculum left schools with little time or inclination to give a high priority to the affective dimension' (Lang 1999: 24). According to Lang, it was when secondary-modern schools and grammar schools merged to form the new comprehensives that the academic/pastoral split occurred. While the former grammar school headteachers retained the more coveted academic role, the 'dispossessed secondary-modern departmental heads' resorted to 'empire building', defining their pastoral role 'as including a counselling element, though very few had any sort of training' (Lang 1999: 25). If trained counsellors were appointed, these 'house heads' saw it as a challenge and an imposition and sought to get rid of them. It is to these 'significant political and ideological dimensions' that Lang attributes the failure of any impact of so-called counselling in developing 'emotional intelligence' among pupils in Britain. More specifically, careers education and guidance suffered a lasting detriment when counselling was marginalized.

Lang also provides a clue as to why the PSE provision in schools has often become irrelevant to pupil needs. The methodology of providing PSE or pastoral care in schools 'is either ignored or treated very simplistically' (1999: 28):

> Concern at the moment seems to be focusing on what the PSE curriculum should include not how it should be delivered. If pupils do not know how to discuss their feelings and those things that really concern them, or do not feel secure enough to do so, even the best possible PSE curriculum will be ineffective, and the door of even the most skilled counsellor may never be reached.

Lang criticizes the mechanistic approach to teacher training enshrined in 'new standards for achieving qualified teacher status' (DfEE 1998e). Such a 'narrow and ideological view of teaching . . . will sideline those vital affective dimensions of education to which counselling contributes' (1999: 24).

ADULT GUIDANCE

While enough has been said about the school context, what is the contribution of those from outside the school system for counselling in careers guidance, for example, the Careers Service?

The only postgraduate qualification within the guidance field has for quite some time been the Diploma in Careers Guidance. This has always been a qualification validated by the local government management board. Currently a new revised modular course is offered by some higher education institutions as a part-time course and through distance learning modes, although the final part of the diploma can only be completed in the field under supervision. The Association of Graduate Careers Advisory Services (AGCAS) has also developed a new Certificate and Diploma in Careers Guidance in Higher Education. Until the 1990s only about '35–40% of AGCAS members [had] a Diploma in Careers Guidance and previous experience of careers work in the wider community' (Ford and Graham 1994: 127). It is a pity that counselling still struggles to become a core skill rather than an elective, since it is the 'hard' skills like job knowledge that can be measured rather than the 'soft' skills of interpersonal sensitivity.

Although CAMPAG has finally come up with a blueprint for generic counselling competences, they offer no clear and unambiguous answers to questions posed by Rivis in 1996. For example:

- What is the likely impact of introducing competence-based occupational standards in a field which is characterised by its emphasis on interpersonal, rather than cognitive, or practical skills?
- How far is it possible to arrive at widely accepted occupational standards for advice, guidance and counselling when there is no agreement about definitions and boundaries, and the field covers a wide range of professional and non-professional practice in an enormous range of disparate work and voluntary settings?
- How far can ethical positions and strong professional value systems be reflected in occupational standards in this field? Can common occupational standards encompass widely differing ethical positions?

(Rivis 1996: 5)

It is exactly the above kind of uncertainties regarding the status of counselling straddling the social sciences and the humanities that delayed the establishment of the Counselling Psychology Division of the British Psychological Society (BPS). Presently the BPS is also struggling with the issue of deciding on criteria for training and accreditation of psychologists 'specialising in formal psychotherapy' (BPS internal working document).

One of the levers of change for the adoption of competence-based occupational standards in counselling/psychotherapy and guidance for training and work, is the European Union's General Systems Directive (1991) on mutual recognition of qualifications among member states. There is also pressure for statutory registration of practitioners in the field. The need for setting national targets for education and training is another imperative with implications for vocational guidance and counselling for an increasingly wider section of the population of all age groups. The following comment spells out this need:

the British workforce is relatively underskilled and underqualified compared to other countries . . . while the UK's academic elite is world-class, it is essential to raise further the level of attainment of the majority of the workforce of all ages. The

labour market is undergoing structural change, in terms both
of supply (fewer young people, more adults) and of demand
(decrease in unskilled manual and clerical jobs) ... there is
high unemployment among those with fewer qualifications
while skill shortages hamper economic renewal.

(Oakshott 1996: 21)

Nevertheless, even as recently as May 1999, an Internet entry for
the DfEE with the heading 'Finding advice and guidance services,
and quality standards & quality assurance for education, training
and career planning (UK)' begins by stating:

In the UK, it is not easy to find advice & guidance, especially if
you are not in a school, college or university. The government
is planning to support more local information, advice and guidance centres for adults *& is currently consulting on the issue*.

(italics in the original)

Again, the emphasis is on advice and guidance with no recognition of the need for counselling for such an undefined and diverse
target population.

It has been said repeatedly that we live in a global knowledge
economy and that information is now the basic raw material of
wealth production. In the fast-disappearing industrial age, life was
easily segmented into the 'learning years' (up to 16 for the majority
and the early 20 for others), the 'earning years' (up to 60 for
women and 65 for men), and the 'yearning years' (on pension or
on social security until demise). Most people, even if they changed
jobs, remained more or less in the same trade, profession or career
until retirement. This is no longer possible. On average, in industrialized societies, most workers are currently said to change careers
five times during their working life, while change of jobs occurs
no less than 14 times. Another statistic of note is that knowledge
doubles every two or three years with 30 to 50 per cent of it becoming obsolete every year in a wide range of work. There is no
more security of lifelong employment; instead there has to be lifelong learning in order to remain employable. In a competitive, fast-
changing marketplace the worker must continue to invest in skills
and knowledge for themselves to avert the danger of becoming
unemployable. In these circumstances, the counselling component
in careers guidance, at least at transition points, including spells
out of work, becomes ever more critical.

Without using the words 'counselling' or even 'interview' the
extract below describes 'a successful and innovative adult guidance

initiative on Merseyside . . . funded through Merseyside's Objective One (European Social Fund) programme' (Farley and Walsh 1998: 26). These are clients who had been unemployed for relatively long periods:

> *Freshstart* is delivered flexibly, the initial step being a one-to-one diagnostic discussion with the client. **The interpersonal skills and experience of the careers advisers are crucial at this stage – their ability to establish rapport and trust are the key to clients' commitment and participation.** The client is offered a menu of activities by the careers adviser which includes:
>
> * confidence building/assertiveness training;
> * skills analysis;
> * occupational analysis including psychometric testing;
> * c.v. preparation;
> * job search skills;
> * individual guidance.
>
> (emphasis in the original)

Although clothed in different terminology the authors clearly recognize the importance of counselling skills as the crucial ingredient in the project's success.

A Learning Information Project run by the same careers company in partnership with the Liverpool City Council and Merseyside Training Enterprise Council (TEC) reports that the work was 'painfully slow'. The target group, unemployed parents of school-age children, was:

> willing to talk about their own experiences [of learning], all negative, however, with few exceptions they were not prepared to take the next step of participation in any group activity or learning opportunity. It was clear that the internal barriers of long term exclusion and negative personal experience were stronger than any external barriers to learning . . . Tackling long term exclusion and disaffection is very resource intensive and relies heavily on personal contact. Breaking down barriers of low self-esteem and confidence is harder than tackling the external barriers of provision.
>
> (Walsh 1999: 8)

This is clearly very similar to the agenda of a counselling interview. There appears to be no better argument than this example for providing proper careers counselling by trained and accredited counsellors in similar situations throughout Britain rather than to rely entirely on 'the personality and effectiveness of the Project Manager, who lived in the area and was trusted' (Walsh 1999: 8). The problem is underlined in the phrase 'very resource intensive' which is jargon for saying that there really is not enough funding for introducing counselling.

GOVERNMENT ACTION

There still remain important initiatives that the government is taking to implement a lifelong learning strategy to combat 'large-scale unemployment' in an era of 'rapid technological change' (Clayton 1999: 13). The two most important are the University for Industry (UfI) with a network of learning centres and local information and guidance (IAG) partnerships that are expected to involve local statutory, community and voluntary agencies. Additionally, a strategic body, the Lifelong Learning Partnership has been launched. This encourages the development of local targets linked to the new national targets for education and training (NTET). It aims to build on and bring together all existing post-16 and lifelong learning arrangements. The minimum (core) partners in Lifelong Learning Partnerships are: further education sector colleges, local authorities and schools, Training Enterprise Councils and careers services. The aim is 'to create a more coherent, effective and accessible set of local arrangements for learning, careers advice and guidance, student support etc.' (CRAC/NICEC Conference Briefing 1999).

The *National Adult Learning Survey 1997* (Benart and Smith 1998) gathered baseline 'information about the learning that a representative sample of people aged between 16 and 69 have undertaken in the last three years' (1997: 3). The learning, whether taught or self-directed, formal or non-formal (on-the-job), job-related or voluntary, or totally non-work, were all included in the survey. It 'involved 5653 computer assisted interviews undertaken with a representative sample of adults [*sic*] aged 16–69 in England and Wales' (1997: 5).

It is useful to look at a summary of Section 11.1 of the main report under the heading 'Career or education advice and guidance'. Even allowing for demographic differences within subsamples it is worrying that the local careers service (65 per cent) along with the Jobcentre (55 per cent) and the Jobclub (63 per cent) was not considered useful as much as guidance received from a place of employment (91 per cent), a college/university (85 per cent), or a Training Enterprise Council (83 per cent).

A quarter (24%) of respondents had received career or education advice or guidance in the past three years (or since leaving
continuous full-time education if this was more recent) from
one or more of a presented list of sources. 33% of learners and
6% of non-learners had received such advice and guidance.
The most frequently cited source of guidance for learners were
employers (17%), a college or university (9%), and a Jobcentre
or UBO (6%). The most frequently cited source for non-learners
was the Jobcentre or UBO (3%).

(Benart and Smith 1998: 27)

The statistics suggest that there was more educational guidance
than careers guidance offered or available to the 24 per cent of
respondents, although the report does not make this distinction
explicit. While 85 per cent of the learners reported that they found
the advice and guidance useful, only 57 per cent of non-learners
did so. Although no one so far appears to have bothered to draw
such an inference, there cannot be a worse indictment of the system (if there is one at all) of adult careers guidance in the United
Kingdom, than the above information published in a recent bench-
mark survey on adult learning (Benart and Smith 1998).

ROLE CONFUSION?

A senior university careers adviser speaking informally with the
author at *The Sunday Times* sponsored Personal Development Show
(4–6 June 1999) spotlighted the difficulties in offering careers counselling within the constraints of a higher education careers guidance
interview. Usually advice and information is given in groups where
much of it is in the form of self-directed, interactive, computer-
assisted packages. University careers advisers are not specifically
trained in personal counselling, and if within the allocated time of
the single careers interview, any personal issues surface, they are
expected to refer the client to external or internal counsellors/
therapists of the university. Confidentiality issues prevent any
liaison between the two agencies and there is no follow-up. From
her account, careers guidance in higher education in the United
Kingdom appears to be very much a hit or miss affair based on
little more than information brokering.

 Butcher *et al.* (1998) in their survey of the entire scene of *Higher
Education Guidance and Counselling Services in the UK* reveal the unco-
ordinated and fragmented nature of what is offered as counselling
in careers guidance. They say that even

in the traditional guidance tasks of individual counselling there is . . . a great disparity in provision . . . Much has been written about the nature and processes of the guidance interview and there is a general consensus that the interaction should be student-centred. There is however, little agreement among practitioners about the role of information giving and how directive or not the interaction should be.

(Butcher *et al.* 1998: 23–4)

Conceptual confusion is evident when they add: 'In the UK, Careers Advisers would not normally refer to such processes [i.e. what happens in the guidance interview] as "counselling" but neither is the interaction always at the level of information giving or advice'. In their view, although careers advisers are not expected to 'offer a therapeutic relationship', they are still expected to have 'highly developed counselling skills and ethics in their general approach' (Butcher *et al.* 1998: 24).

There is also lack of clarity in the demarcation of helping roles in higher education. Discussing counselling services as distinct from careers services, Butcher *et al.* go on to say: 'the personal cannot be divorced from the vocational so that all counsellors at some time find themselves working therapeutically with the psychological aspects of a student's career choice. It is recognised that this is not the main focus of the work but it is an inevitable part' (1998: 29). It is as if the careers adviser offers reluctant or out-of-role personal counselling to the student, while his or her personal counsellor offers similar services in the career domain. All the while the two professionals are prevented from communicating with each other due to organizational and perceived ethical boundaries, not to speak of an element of professional rivalry.

Butcher *et al.* describe a model offered as a 'student-centred holistic guidance model' (Van Esbroeck and Watts 1997) which still distinguishes among three types of guidance: educational, vocational, and personal. As hinted above, the holistic nature of the model breaks down when Butcher *et al.* (1998: 30) report:

There is a clear division between therapeutic counselling services and careers guidance services. Despite the fact that an influential source for the development of student counselling in Britain was the combined careers counselling service at Keele University . . . careers guidance and counselling have each developed their own professional identity and there are currently few formal links between the two professions. This is despite general agreement that there are common issues, not least the ethical framework within which each work.

THE PRACTICE OF CAREERS COUNSELLING

Nevertheless, there are examples of good counselling practice in this setting. For example, one careers adviser of an adult careers guidance facility still managed directly by a local authority in south-east England, undertook part-time training in Integrative and Humanistic Counselling so that she could better serve her clients' needs.

Within the overall policy imperative of economic regeneration of less affluent and neglected parts of the county, Jane (not her real name) is a member of a team of three full-time and three part-time careers advisers (all women) who are free to use their expertise and personal strengths to effect changes to improve the lives of adult residents who seek their help. While they operate from a shopfront drop-in facility, some clients are referred by the Employment Service under the New Deal and the Welfare to Work schemes. Jane is the only person in the centre with training in counselling, and by informal agreement receives the clients with an identified need for 'confidence building', or anyone whose problems appear more than just lack of paid work. She does not keep notes except for bare facts for administrative purposes and the counselling offered is one-to-one and totally confidential. No report is prepared, but in rare instances an action plan may be produced jointly with the client.

Jane finds it professionally distressing that a large proportion of the unemployed have lost their jobs due to various problems unrelated to their skills or capacity to work. They come voluntarily with the declared aim of finding another job, career or retraining, but often it is either their inability to get on with their former boss or colleagues, or any number of extraneous reasons that have contributed to their problems. Once Jane has won their trust, and because they are allowed more than just the usual one or two meetings with her, she is able to get closer to their concerns. She and they can then begin to address these concerns collaboratively.

One example is a woman who came in with the request for information on careers in social work. However, this woman's emotional state and non-verbal clues suggested to the member of staff on the information desk the need to refer her to Jane. Jane realized that the woman was 'bursting to say something to her, but was also holding back'. She allowed space and time for the woman to assess her trustworthiness and revealed that she, a mother of a toddler, had been claiming benefit while engaged in 'odd jobs'. This resulted in being detected and consequently losing entitlement to benefit. She was desperate to find work. Jane also discovered that the woman was a 'battered wife' living in a refuge and since she now needed to earn a living, had thought that her role of unpaid assistant to social workers at the refuge, which she enjoyed, would qualify her to find a similar job in open employment. She had no idea of the years of training and the stringent entry qualifications needed to rise above the level of voluntary helper. It took months of once-a-week counselling to first uncover her co-dependent role with her violent and alcohol-abusing husband before she could take effective steps to set a viable career goal within her admittedly limited potential at the time. Much more important for this woman was that, by developing a working alliance with Jane, she was able to define herself as a person independent of her predicament, and to gain immeasurably in self-esteem. Without this as a foundation it was unlikely that she would have benefited from any of a range of activities routinely offered as adult careers guidance.

Jane believes that if her work, which she modestly says is not very different from her colleagues who have intuitively developed a similar approach, was to be publicly announced as 'counselling', most of her voluntary clients would avoid her like the plague. She says that she 'plays the counselling card close to her chest'. She also believes that in Britain public perception of counselling is largely connected with inadequacy, mental ill health and the often much publicized medico-legal invasions into people's private lives against their will. This probably explains why counselling in Britain, unless it is the kind resorted to by the elite, is often a shadowy enterprise lacking in scientific or academic prestige, engaged in by volunteers or regarded as an alternative (or complementary) treatment akin to hypnotherapy.

Jane tells of two New Deal clients referred by the Employment Service to the local authority funded adult careers guidance facility where she works. The New Deal is a government initiative whereby young unemployed persons are allowed up to four months on a 'Gateway' programme to access 'in-depth guidance and personal development . . . It is client based, with contracts based on the needs of the individual, who moreover have [sic] a choice of guidance service' (Clayton 1999: 167).

The first client had never worked in open employment. He had been in foster care since his parents split up when he was a child. He had recently established contact with his natural father, although he had never met his mother and was unlikely to do so in the future. He had been told by the Jobcentre that he should get himself a c.v.

He despaired because he had no qualifications and no work experience, and as Jane found out, very poor literacy and numeracy skills. He had thought that a c.v. of any kind was utterly beyond him. In the process of counselling this young man, Jane said that she had to act almost as a mother substitute. In fact, she used the phrase 'a good enough mother', to describe her role with this client, a concept borrowed from Winnicott (Winnicott *et al.* 1988) and from developmental psychology.

During their meetings Jane discovered that the young man had undertaken gardening and landscape design as a volunteer spare time activity. He had learnt, by being shown, how to measure and weigh quantities, mix cement and sand to different consistencies to make concrete, how to erect fences and other similar tasks. He then began to realize that he was not entirely without skills and was able to use his own words to put down his competencies on paper. Having got to this stage he was able to write speculative letters to prospective employers.

Another young man was a very shy and withdrawn individual. He had been with a firm where he had worked alone at a computer console, inputting data. The work kept piling up and he felt unable to cope. He had not learnt to prioritize work. Instead of letting his supervisor know of his difficulties, he had simply quit. Since then he had given up any hope of returning to work, believing that his past failure to hold down a job would be known to prospective employers, and that this would immediately disqualify him.

It took a few more weekly meetings before Jane was able to gently confront and challenge this young man on his irrational beliefs. Starting with a humanistic, accepting, and 'unconditional positive regard' approach, Jane moved on to a form of brief cognitive behavioural therapy, before she could help him overcome his sense of shame and failure. He then improved upon his earlier unkempt appearance and began to be offered interviews. He was able to talk at interviews about his past job, and why he gave it up, without being shame-faced, fearful and apologetic.

It is not only the young without readily marketable skills or social skills who have problems in the job market. Older workers with recognized skills who had once expected they would remain in the same firm, doing more or less the same job until retirement, sense that they are on the scrap heap when faced with involuntary redundancy. Unaware of the inexorable and continuing changes in the labour market, most of them become 'discouraged workers', unable to adapt to the new circumstances. As Clayton (1999: 13) observes:

many employers are now looking for skills other than the job-specific: foundation skills such as reading, writing, listening and speaking; creative thinking, decision-making, problem-solving, learning; and display of responsibility, self-esteem, self-management and integrity; and key competencies such as planning and organising, interpersonal skills, information use, understanding of complex systems and familiarity with a range of technology.

Clayton adds that although 'the state *Employment Service* (ES) offers information and advice to the unemployed and a specialised service for disabled people, [it] does not claim to be a holistic, client-centred guidance and counselling service' (1999: 169). She also acknowledges that: 'Adults need a holistic approach, which takes account [of] many other circumstances, such as age, health and family. Their possibilities may be more constrained and the time scale for action shorter than for many young people' (1999: 15). Her conclusion is:

> In Britain, despite the great complexity of programmes . . . and despite many recommendations from various bodies on the increased need for guidance and labour market information, there is no statutory provider of vocational guidance open to all adults and guidance remains marginalized and under-funded. The ideal of lifelong careers guidance to support lifelong career development is very far from being met.

And,

> A major problem for adult disadvantaged groups seeking to compete in today's rapidly changing labour market is that independent vocational guidance and counselling, with tried and tested methods for facilitating entry to education, training and employment, has a low profile, is not uniformly available and is often hard to access.
>
> (Clayton 1999: 169, 176)

FURTHER EXAMPLES

I conclude this chapter with my own growing use and understanding of counselling as of central importance in the assessment and guidance of a wide cross-section of adults in careers work. During most of the 1980s as an occupational psychologist with the state employment service, I successively worked at two Employment

Rehabilitation Centres (ERCs) for the disabled and the disadvantaged. Modelled on Government Training Centres or Skillcentres
with which the premises were often shared, the ERCs employed
trade instructors who assessed disabled clients in various practical
activities ranging from assembly tasks to bench joinery, machine
shop work and office technology.

Within the 26 ERCs scattered throughout Britain, psychologists
were essentially charged with interviewing and allocating clients
to the various work sections, often using cognitive tests or work
samples to support their decisions. A social worker was expected
to attend to any personal problems that the client presented. A medical doctor or nurse was on site to monitor medication or indicate
limitations imposed by disability, and usually attended the weekly
case conference discussing the progress of clients. A final report
written by the psychologist with recommendations approved by the
case conference would be sent to the Disablement Resettlement
Officer (DRO) at the Jobcentre network. The clients appeared to have
very little say in the proceedings, except in those rare instances
when someone decided to be 'awkward'. Of course, all this activity
in the postindustrial era was eventually seen as an anachronism
and quickly disappeared in the 1990s with hardly anything else
to replace it. However, the present Labour government appears to
be taking various new initiatives to help those disadvantaged in the
labour market.

One of my first clients was a young man of 22, who had been
referred by his local DRO with the information that he suffered
from epilepsy, and that he had never worked. A medical report
obtained from his GP briefly summarized his medical history. Until
recently he had been overweight (nearly 20 stone) but with the
help of a dietician had reduced to 11 stone. He was still obviously
wearing his old clothes, since his jacket hung loosely on him and
his trousers were baggy. He seemed unable to focus his pale blue
eyes and looked about him with a vague expression. The story that
this young man told me at the interview was so out of the ordinary,
that a psychologist's standard tools of tests and assessments, and a
six-week stay at the ERC could hardly have begun to address his
concerns and needs.

Born and brought up in a council flat in Bow, Adam Smith (not
his real name) had never been to school. His father was a butcher
and had married his mother when she worked on the till at the
butcher's shop. They were both pretty well advanced in years when
Adam was born, their only offspring. While his mother stayed at
home, the father worked long hours, six days a week. Mother

devoted herself totally to keeping house, and of course, to their only child. They had no visitors, neither relations nor friends, and they never went anywhere. Once a week his mother would shop locally and that was the only time Adam got out of the house. He was told that danger lurked among outsiders and that the family should keep to themselves. When confronted by other curious children, he literally hid behind his mother's skirt. Their only window to the outside world was a television set.

On the very first day that Adam was taken to primary school by his mother, he cried so much and made such a nuisance of himself that the headteacher suggested a special school for him. But the authorities totally lost sight of him and he never attended an educational establishment of any kind during his childhood.

Adam stayed at home, watched TV, and learned to read and write from his mother. His father was left out of the secret that he was not attending school. He was not taught arithmetic. He could write English (capital letters) but his letters were at least five times as large as ordinary manuscript. Adam's mother encouraged him to watch the 'more refined' programmes, and not surprisingly, his diction and speech were almost BBC standard. His reading matter consisted of fantastic tales of the supernatural and science fiction, bought by his mother. He had his own room. He ate whatever his mother prepared for him, did not do anything physical, least of all exercise, and grew enormously fat. According to Adam, his mother bathed him, even into his 20s. He was self-contained within the mother–son dyad with father at the periphery, growing old and too tired to get involved. At the time Adam attended the ERC, his father, who was soon to die, was 80 years old and his mother was approaching 70.

Since Adam was almost totally illiterate except within his circumscribed fantasy world, and also innumerate, no established psychometric tests could be used to assess his potential. Everyone else at the first case conference wanted to terminate Adam's stay at the ERC and recommend that he seek work as a trolley retriever at a supermarket, or do simple repetitive work of a similar nature. I was the only exception, taking a view that he should stay longer, if only to expose him to social realities outside his mostly unintentionally dysfunctional nuclear family. I persuaded the ERC manager to extend Adam's stay up to six months, which he did, invoking some special dispensation clause peculiar to the Civil Service.

Adam's reclusive existence was disturbed one day when his mother suddenly fell ill and fainted. He had enough wit to dial 999 and ask for an ambulance. The ambulance crew, who appeared from nowhere like Martians, took his mother away to St Thomas's hospital. The following day, surprisingly, prompted by an elderly woman neighbour, Adam took a bus for the first time in his life to get to the hospital to see his sick mother. The mother had appreciably recovered, and spoke to him from her bed. The nurses, enchanted beings, were kind to Adam. He was too frightened to take the lift, but he boarded the right bus and got home all right. He repeated the exploit of visiting the hospital twice more and noticed that the doctors and nurses were not enemy aliens but allies in their concern for his mother's and even his own health.

A few months later, Adam suffered his first 'epileptic fit' which got him into the same hospital attended by similar nurses and a doctor who came to know of his peculiar situation and treated him extremely kindly. He was put under the care of a dietician and was sent to King's College hospital for dental treatment since he had never bothered to brush his teeth before. It is only after a year or so of medical treatment that he was declared fit (as he was now chronologically an adult) to seek suitable employment.

By then, Hans Eysenck (1961) had purged psychology of the 'poetic' and 'fictional' influence of Freud. It was striving to be an exact science. The psychologist as the expert would test, tell, and allocate individuals to appropriate vocational training and activities. Professor Alec Rodgers's Seven Point Plan and his Fitting Man to the Job and Fitting Job to the Man (FMJ–FJM) model held sway in occupational psychology. When I began to look for alternative paradigms in counselling and therapy, the government chief psychologist told me angrily to leave such nonsense to the social workers. However much I tried, what I had learnt in my training was to no avail in helping Adam, and scores of others, who did not fit any official model of the disabled job seeker.

At my own expense and my own time, usually evenings and weekends, I treated myself to a smorgasbord of counselling and therapy skills, even enlisting myself in a co-counselling group. I do not know how effective I was with Adam with my embryonic counselling skills, but I spent a great deal of time with him listening to his story without judging, condemning or advising. Some instructors at the ERC also took an interest in him and taught him joined up writing and the four basic rules of arithmetic. He learnt social skills through welcoming newcomers and escorting visitors around the premises. He was well-spoken, and he got on well with most people. I visited him once at his home and met his stereotypical Oedipal mother. He in turn visited me at home once and had lunch with my family. He wrote me a couple of letters after he left the ERC. His local authority social services department helped him acquire GCE (O and A level) qualifications which enabled him to read philosophy at university, and I heard later that he gained an Upper Second Class Honours degree. When I last heard of him he was employed by a local council in a temporary clerical job. Sadly though he had not yet escaped from his mother's toxic, emotional dominance.

Five years later, with more experience in counselling, I experienced the unexpected success of counselling a woman labelled schizophrenic who showed symptoms after sudden withdrawal from regular medication. Mrs McDonald (not her real name) was in her 40s, recently divorced by her dentist husband and housed in single accommodation. She was the mother of two daughters at university. She had been forbidden contact with them. For quite some time during the marriage, her husband had sought to conceal the facts regarding her mental illness for fear of the stigma attaching to himself. When it could no longer be concealed, she was divorced with a small settlement, and she ended up in a mental hospital. She had been forcibly medicated, but she rebelled and left the hospital of her own accord. She would not take medication. Wanting desperately to find employment using secretarial skills that she claimed she had developed prior to marriage, she approached the Jobcentre. Since she had no recent record of work, and had been ill, the DRO referred her for assessment at the ERC.

The male instructor required to instruct and assess her employability using office skills, flatly refused to have her in his section. That was not surprising since she could hardly sit still. When seated she would cross and uncross her legs continuously or pace up and down the room when unable to sit any longer. The manager sought my advice before terminating her assessment. I asked for two more weeks, and was allowed to transfer her to a clerical section run by a sympathetic woman instructor. I listened to Mrs McDonald's life history with great care, and prepared a tape in the form of a legendary fable, which paralleled her story in its most significant features, ending in triumph for the protagonist through overcoming all odds. My rationale was the direct access to the unconscious that story-telling is supposed to induce. It could speak to her story at one remove, and in its positive ending support her ego-strength. (Story-telling and the narrative approach to counselling in careers guidance are discussed in detail elsewhere in this book.) She was to listen to the tape as often as she needed to at home, especially before retiring as well as first thing in the morning. Within two days she ceased to show withdrawal symptoms and buckled down to brushing up her typing and shorthand. She left the ERC the following week and was employed as a part-time secretary. Later she re-established contact with her former husband and travelled with him to see her daughter at the university.

I delivered a paper on this case to the British Psychological Society Occupational Psychology Conference (1986). It was dismissed as unacceptable, not meeting standards of scientific rigour. My work with this client was seen as a one-off, an N=1 experiment, not replicable and therefore not worthy of serious professional attention. However, I continued with my experimentation with various counselling models and had demonstrable successes with individual clients.

More recently I have been working with disabled ex-servicemen and women using a wide range of psychometric tests in their vocational assessment. I have continued with counselling as the means of establishing rapport and building a working alliance over a three-day period of assessment. Every ex-service person reveals an interesting narrative of their life-career, not just those who have seen active service, whether in Northern Ireland, the Falklands, the Persian Gulf, or in former Yugoslavia. Those who have left some years ago and have struggled with the invariably painful resocialization process of adjusting to the unfamiliar terrain of civilian work life, often have other, less glamorous stories to tell. Many have not been listened to with any semblance of care or respect by anyone they have met in the course of their transition to civilian life. Once out of work, they have been at the mercy of bureaucrats, or busy professionals, including medical doctors, who have had neither time, interest, nor sympathy, let alone the empathy they crave in their marginalized status.

Living on meagre state benefits, minimal war pensions, or intermittent charitable handouts, on first contact, they often reveal complicated domestic pressures and problems. They may display a sense of grievance, anger or frustration. Their presenting problems range from protracted negotiations with various authorities or institutions regarding benefits, insurance, rent, mortgage, child custody, childcare and matrimonial matters and concerns. Often there is unresolved court action or litigation surrounding any of the above. At interview some present obvious psychological symptoms of stress, anxiety and depression.

In offering vocational assessment and career guidance to the ex-serviceman and woman, it is clear that providing a counselling milieu where they can in a few hourly sessions express the wrenching emotions, and look more deeply at themselves, is essential to empower them, and enable them to make sense of the situations in which they find themselves.

The careers officer Jane (see pp. 83–5) and myself are just two examples of people working in this field who felt the need for counselling training of some kind and have been able to adapt it to the careers and guidance setting. Some colleagues have proved supportive, and valued this aspect of the work. Others have been suspicious and critical of emotions being given more attention than facts. The wide range of professional relationships and networks that the career guidance practitioner must increasingly negotiate forms the subject matter of the next chapter.

· FIVE ·

Professional relationships in counselling in careers guidance

Assessment and the provision of information that ensure the immediate objective of integrating or reintegrating an individual into the job market may still be seen as the primary objective of careers guidance. However, the establishment or restoration of autonomy, confidence, and personal and professional growth, which maximizes a person's potential, is the indispensable added value that counselling contributes to careers guidance. The case studies briefly outlined in the previous chapter clearly attest to this. It is suggested that, from a systems point of view, optimum outcomes may be achieved through a network of contact among a range of social, economic, and institutional actors. However, the family and community support system, the educational and vocational training system, and the enterprise and labour market system, are not always linked in the most identifiable or effective ways.

The agencies through which careers guidance is offered (with varying degrees of counselling) have been identified as:

- the Careers Service which used to be run by local education authorities and is now largely privatized;
- careers programmes run by careers coordinators and other tutors in schools and colleges of further education;
- careers services in universities, and colleges of higher education.

Additionally, there are:

- educational guidance services for adults (EGSA);
- private, fee-charging careers guidance services and, voluntary, charitable institutions.

Increasingly, employers use assessment and development centres and employee assistance programmes as ongoing measures of career and personal counselling offered to a flexible workforce.

In the interface between the individual and paid employment, the influence of family, relations, friends and peers traditionally accounts for at least the initial level of aspiration and choice for most entrants to the job market. Even so, the Careers Service reportedly influences a quarter of postschool choices. As examined in the previous chapter, for most adults career change, or re-entry into the job market after illness, disability, migration or family responsibilities can become something of a lottery. The job market is increasingly uncertain, volatile and unpredictable, and not easily comprehended through a previous generation's first-hand experience alone. The relationships, partnerships, and networking alliances between and among various key players in and outside the agencies listed above are therefore crucial in providing an effective, accessible and seamless service expected in modern careers counselling and guidance provision.

With the privatization of the careers service, the service level agreements it had with individual schools are succeeded by partnership agreements left for each of the parties to negotiate within statutory guidelines. This gives access for careers advisers to designated staff, pupils and their records within the school, where they have the broader responsibility of disseminating information on jobs and careers. The Careers Service establishes regular contacts with local employers who notify vacancies as they arise. It also compiles destination data. In 1998, under a central government funding initiative, careers libraries were installed in many secondary schools by the respective careers companies with support from regional Training Enterprise Councils.

WIDENING THE REMIT

In this chapter I begin by exploring the way in which professional relationships are extended in providing careers guidance to those at risk of social exclusion who appear to be the focus of current government concern. There is a growing fear that the proportion of economically active persons at risk of job loss is increasing in almost all postindustrial societies. The trend is towards more 'contingent' or casual workers with the proportion of part-time workers also increasing. Even for those in full-time work, tenure is uncertain (Collin and Watts 1996: 389). Hutton (1995) sees evidence for what he terms the 30/30/40 society. According to him, as much as 30 per cent of the population is disadvantaged, jobless, and live without hope of improving their situation. Another 30 per cent are marginalized in that they are insecure in their jobs and enjoy few long-term benefits. Only about 40 per cent of the population, the privileged, develop the necessary knowledge, skills and attitudes to hold down secure jobs, or to become gainfully self-employed.

Watts (1999) argues that such a scenario confines careers work to the 'bureaucratic sectors of the labour market' excluding what he terms the 'entrepreneurial sector'. He advocates informal or community-based guidance interventions by co-opting 'non formal guidance agents who are more likely to have the contacts, the credibility, and the "street knowledge"' (1999: 21). Watts (1999: 24) identifies these informal, often volunteer guidance agents as:

> those operating in a professional role to which a guidance element can be added. The latter include youth and community workers, social workers, health workers, and those in religious organisations. Some may be based in community-based *agencies* with a broad remit to offer a range of information, advice and support services to clients; or in community-based *programmes* such as family learning centres, family literacy schemes, neighbourhood projects, and community education projects.

To this list one could add those workers in cultural institutions and organizations involved in popular arts, the media and the theatre. Watts (1999: 26) goes even so far as to suggest that careers counselling and guidance should define its purposes more broadly, supporting 'individuals to achieve viable and socially legitimate lifestyles outside the formal systems'.

The government has announced a 'radical new response' scheduled to be phased in over a two- to three-year period from April 2001 called 'The Connexions Service'. It is a strategy of inclusion aimed at the teenage population not in education, employment or training, professedly developed in consultation with young people themselves. Adult mentors recruited into 'a new profession of Personal Advisers' are expected to be 'drawn from a range of backgrounds including the Careers Service, Youth Service, Social Services, teachers and Youth Offending Teams, as well as from the voluntary and community sectors' (DfEE: 45). Again, although the word was not used, there is little doubt that the role of 'Personal Adviser' encompasses counselling. There was 'general agreement' that a personal adviser should be someone that a 'young person can get to know and trust, and who will understand their needs', and 'someone who is prepared to act in an advocacy role for the young person' (p. 56).

A project reported as 'Guidance for the Millennium' (Norris 1999) funded by the EU Single Regeneration Budget involving five London boroughs (Bexley, Greenwich, Lewisham, Newham and Tower Hamlets) developed a unique partnership with three separate careers companies (London South Bank Careers, Prospects (South) Careers Services, and Futures Careers Guidance). Their outreach work extended to youth centres, adult education venues, job centres, community groups, women's projects, one-stop shops and various other community organizations. The client group was overwhelmingly diverse in terms of 'ethnicity, education, life experience, age and starkly high levels of disadvantage and deprivation, e.g. mental and physical health problems, poverty [and] discrimination' (*Newscheck* 1999: 18). One of the conclusions was that although much 'time and effort are needed to network properly, the positive outcomes for advisers and clients have been demonstrated' (*Newscheck* 1999: 18).

The need for counselling was highlighted by the recognition of a 'much stronger demand for individual, one-to-one guidance (rather than in groups) from disadvantaged people with limited self-confidence' (*Newscheck* 1999: 18). One client's response to the feedback questionnaire sums up this need and how well it was met.

I found the care and compassion outstanding, the professionalism of the 'Careers Adviser' who spent time listening and the degree of perception for my needs, not only as someone seeking work and advice but as a human being – excellent . . . all credit to her.
                              (*Newscheck* 1999: 18, original italicized)

Many more similar feedback responses from the clients were reported. The project organizers, while congratulating themselves on a job well done in taking on board the hitherto unmet needs of those marginalized, at risk of social exclusion or those described as the 'disengaged', do not necessarily appear to have paid sufficient attention to the implications for a changed emphasis in staff training to include counselling.

The Institute of Career Guidance initiated a Mentoring Action Project (MAP) funded under the European Commission's Youthstart Programme to provide careers guidance to 'disengaged' young people. The NICEC/ICG Briefing Paper (1998) begins 'Careers services are being encouraged by government to prioritise guidance work with disengaged target groups, and to introduce policies which minimise the numbers of young people who drop out of education and training.' A mentoring approach to careers guidance was piloted (MAP) followed by a further initiative labelled 'Stepping Stones'. Mentors are not professionals but ordinary people who are described as those 'who, through their action and work, help others to achieve their potential'. However, what is described as mentoring in career guidance appears no different from counselling best practice. The briefing lays down as 'conditions for success' that mentors must 'develop additional skills' to:

- enter the client's frame of reference;
- help clients to understand their potential to change;
- provide interactive feedback on change;
- open doors (through advocacy and negotiation) and cross thresholds with clients in ways which support rather than disempower them.

(NICEC/ICG 1998)

Why the Institute of Career Guidance is unwilling to identify most of the above activities as 'counselling' is a mystery, especially when one reads the following under the term *Agape* (explained as a Greek word meaning genuine charity and selflessness of service):

External evaluation shows that successful mentors attain high standards in terms of client-centredness, depth of empathy and understanding, and knowledge of their clients. The mentors concerned demonstrate a genuine client-centred concern and caring for each individual client, which is warm, dispassionate, spontaneous, and non-judgemental, and with a readiness to go an 'additional mile' beyond the normal call of duty.

(NICEC/ICG 1998: unpaginated – third page)

There is no better evidence for the counselling basis of mentoring than when the document declares, 'the function of the mentor as role model may lie largely in the *unconscious* of both mentors and mentees' (NICEC/ICG 1998: last page, my emphasis).

Effective partnerships with other voluntary or statutory agencies are at the heart of the initiatives described above. The reasons for the emphasis on partnerships will be examined later.

'Stepping Stones' commenced in 1998 as the second stage of the Youthstart mentoring project, but introduced group work instead of individual mentoring, mainly one suspects, for reasons of economy. This initiative was reported as *Career Guidance and Socially Excluded Young People: Working with Groups* (ICG Briefing, undated). Apart from sole delivery by a Stepping Stones worker, a number of other partnership models of delivery were also tried out. These included:

- career guidance inputs with 'primary responsibility by another local partner' (e.g. the Prince's Trust and Feltham Young Offender's institution);
- delivery on a 'team basis with another main partner' (e.g. 'Youth Buzz' mobile outreach project);
- 'mix "n" match provision' with specialist input from other agencies (e.g. St John Ambulance); and
- team delivery (drawing on 'specialists').

(ICG undated a: 2)

An example was of a careers company working with the local Education Business Partnership, and the Youth and Community Service to organize student support clubs which provided 'continuity of activity and support during the transitional period from school until young people are settled in work or learning' (ICG undated a: 2). One specific and typical initiative was a theatre workshop led by a youth worker employed by the Careers Service. Here we see the gradual extension of the concept of careers counselling and guidance to encompass the wider parameters of life-space and life-career, not to speak of lifelong learning, requiring the participation of those whose expertise is outside the traditional areas of careers work.

The importance of counselling is again highlighted, although perversely with no acknowledgement or recognition of it, in the following extract:

> Within the guidance profession a new hybrid area of specialisation would seem to be emerging which calls for a wide range of skills and abilities, some of which may not necessarily be associated with the more traditional functions of the careers service companies . . . it suggests that guidance workers who are successful in work with disengaged young people may not be restricted to any one specific professional background.
>
> Some careers companies have already anticipated this by appointing staff from other backgrounds to specialise in work with disengaged groups. Similarly, career guidance specialists in outreach may be *expected to have specialist interpersonal and relationship skills*.

(Ford 1999: 33, my emphasis)

A European Union project, under the PETRA and LEONARDO programmes and covering six countries (Belgium, Ireland, Netherlands, Portugal, Spain and UK), explored ways of linking formal and non-formal guidance provision. Some of the informal or volunteer vocational guidance and counselling staff were allowed entry as trainees into the formal system. In negotiating the content of the programme with participants (e.g. Conamara, Ireland) it is reported that there was

> a tendency for counselling and group-work elements to dominate the programme, at the expense of more specific guidance elements . . . Similarly, the Portuguese project has tended to focus on personal and social rather than on educational and vocational matters.
>
> (Ford 1999)

However, the briefing also admits that:

> Relationship-building skills, and attention to personal and social matters, provide the essential base on which attention to educational and vocational guidance matters can be built. The balance between the two must be carefully struck.
>
> (Ford 1999: unpaginated, fourth page)

Ford (1999) concludes that the value of the LEONARDO programme may lie in a 'more general sensitising of formal guidance services to the importance of non-formal guidance providers, and to more diverse forms of support for such providers'. It appears even more important that formal guidance providers take on board the unquestionable need and demand for personal counselling in educational and vocational guidance. To some extent this has been acknowledged in *Adult Guidance in Community Settings* (Jackson and Haughton 1998: 2) where it says:

> A major element of guidance delivered through community settings is the emphasis on individual personal development, and the holistic approach to problem-solving and decision-making. Personal development is the platform on which the work is undertaken.

Research had shown (Department of Employment 1981) that employers were uncertain of the responsibilities of the Careers Service and often confused its role with that of the Employment Service Jobcentres. Local employers who relied on the Careers Service to recommend school-leavers for entry-level jobs often complained of inadequate preparation of young people for job interviews. Even before lack of basic skills or lack of experience, they put poor attitude, appearance and manners as reasons for 'dissatisfaction with the quality of referral' (DoE 1981: 13). The employers perceived the job applicants as not 'well briefed' by the careers advisers. Here again, it is difficult to envisage any improvements to the situation if

the Careers Service has not yet taken on board the necessity for
career counselling as opposed to one short guidance interview. During 1998/99 the Careers Service was charged by the government
with the duty of focusing specifically 'upon those who most need
guidance and support to achieve their [vocational] goals' (DfEE
1998c: 1).

> Having conducted five regional workshops, the above report
> concludes: CSs are now far more closely involved with other
> agencies who deal with the 'harder to place' or more vulner-
> able clients and they are spending a lot of effort and resource
> on making these links work effectively. Partnership activity
> appears to be more effective when their [*sic*] are links at both
> strategic and operational levels.

This document cautions, however,

> There can be a problem for CSs caused by having a heightened
> profile in the local community. This arises by being invited to
> join everything even remotely connected with their remit.
> (DfEE 1998c: 8)

Almost all the difficulties that the Careers Service encounters
in identifying the 'at risk' or the 'disaffected' youth, and working
in partnership with other agencies to improve their prospects, are
regarded as due to uncertainties and inadequacies in resources
including competition among partnership agencies for securing
long-term funding. The above report, under the heading *Issues for
DfEE to Consider*, says, 'Some of the necessary activities with the
disaffected do not have any tangible outcome but can be resource
intensive (e.g. mentoring)' (DfEE 1998c: 4). It is curious that there
is no mention of counselling as another possible 'resource intensive
activity' with no 'tangible outcome' but one that clearly must be
included as another 'necessary activity'. However, the report adds
that 'short-termism' leading to 'bolt-on activity' must be condemned
not only just at the level of 'funding methodology' (DfEE 1998c: 7)
but at the level of DfEE strategic thinking as well.

PROFESSIONAL ROLES RELATED TO CAREERS
COUNSELLING IN HIGHER EDUCATION

Watts and Esbroeck (1998) have developed a structural model and
a taxonomy of roles in guidance and counselling services in higher
education that could be applied across the European Union. As

mentioned in Chapter 4, the model is a holistic one with the student at the centre with personal, educational and vocational guidance being offered at three levels labelled 'first-in-line, second-in-line, and third-in-line' (Watts and Esbroeck 1998: 22). While the first-in-line is regarded as part of the formal teaching function and sometimes delivered by paraprofessionals covering all three focuses of guidance, the next level is 'linked to formal teaching but with some degree of specialisation' (1998: 22). The third-in-line is the true professional and specialized function separated from teaching altogether.

Based on what Watts and Esbroeck (1998: 47) call a pragmatic approach, the roles were classified into 14 distinct categories. They are given the labels:

(a) 'first-in-line' adviser;
(b) director (educational and vocational guidance service);
(c) director (psychological counselling service);
(d) study adviser/counsellor;
(e) study and careers counsellor/adviser;
(f) careers counsellor/adviser;
(g) psychological counsellor;
(h) psychiatrist;
(i) social worker;
(j) adviser for students with disabilities;
(k) international adviser;
(l) information officer;
(m) placement officer;
(n) other specialist roles.

These roles are found within a 'taxonomy of services' listed as:

(a) tutorial systems;
(b) decentralised educational guidance services;
(c) centralised educational guidance services;
(d) educational and vocational guidance services;
(e) careers services;
(f) student welfare services;
(g) psychological counselling services;
(h) international offices;
(i) services for students with disabilities;
(j) services for other special groups.

(Watts and Esbroeck 1998: 28)

However, the authors caution that although many of the above titles closely correspond to the taxonomy of services, not all do so: some services encompass a range of roles from different categories. Some roles are 'borderline' and could readily be included in other categories than the ones to which they are assigned.

(Watts and Esbroeck 1998: 47)

Butcher *et al.* (1998) have described at length most tasks performed in the main occupational roles of guidance and counselling at British universities. Some of these roles are briefly discussed below.

A director of Careers Service at a large university may not have a student case-load, instead devoting most of his or her time in managing the service. They may

choose to be involved in information management or the development of vacancy information . . . Some will wish to take a leading role in community guidance networks, feeding back graduate destinations to feeder schools and colleges; others may choose or be required to be directly engaged in the follow-up of graduate destinations.

(Butcher *et al.* 1998: 22)

Careers advisers at universities may or may not have a director as head depending on the numbers employed. Most appear to have given up the traditional face-to-face interview in favour of group work, 'facilitating self-assessment as a general approach' (Butcher *et al.* 1998: 22). However, all careers advisers must 'comply with the first-destination survey of the Higher Education Statistics Agency' (1998: 24) at the end of six months after graduation.

Butcher *et al.* (1998: 24) state:

Internal and external links are likely to be determined by the role and priorities of the Careers Service, although there is scope for individual Careers Advisers to develop personal professional orientations: work with mature students, for example, or with the disabled; guidance by distance learning provision; information provision; or developing specialist knowledge of European opportunities.

The information officer, usually responsible for the careers information room, provides 'students and sometimes Careers Officers with detailed and up-to-date information on occupations, companies, courses and vacancies both permanent and temporary' (Butcher *et al.* 1998: 25). Some universities employ placement officers who obtain information on placement opportunities for students with corporate or individual employers and may pre-select students to fill notified vacancies. For part-time, seasonal or temporary work that students usually take up during vacation, there are likely to be job shop managers who facilitate this through liaison with local employers.

Academics may take on the role of careers tutor offering a 'first-in-line' service since there is less availability of personal tutors in an increasingly overcrowded system of higher education. There is instead a new development with the appointment of Enterprise Managers at '56 universities involved in the Enterprise in Higher Education (EHE) initiative' (Butcher *et al.* 1998: 27). Butcher *et al.* (1998: 27) assert that the

> most enduring role for this practitioner group has been ... supporting developments in departments to enhance the quality of teaching and learning by developing students' personal and transferable skills as well as their discipline-specific knowledge, and ... draw employers into the academic curriculum.

There are other, specific roles that some universities provide as student development officer and international student adviser. Since there is now a requirement for higher education institutions to publish a disability statement there are advisers or coordinators to 'provide guidance on disability issues ... and liaise with a wide variety of external agencies – schools, colleges, other higher education institutions, Local Education Authorities, national [disability] groups' (Butcher *et al.* 1998: 31).

With the Open University, the role of first-in-line teacher/tutor/trainer has been transformed into the 'tutor–counsellor', a rare instance of the use of the term 'counsellor' in guidance in Britain. These tutor–counsellors are mostly part-time and regionally based. As Diane Bailey (1987: 240) observes,

> In open learning models in which the main teaching artery is the package of linked texts, tapes, kits or programs, the tutor is displaced from main subject authority towards the guidance roles of counselling, encouragement, coaching in learning skills and advocacy.

However, there is no requirement that they are trained in personal or careers counselling and are therefore said to be 'highly divergent in their role interpretations' (Bailey 1987: 240). The OU tutor–counsellor is invariably not trained or qualified for the expected role.

As briefly referred to in the previous chapter, personal counselling in higher education in the United Kingdom has developed a
separate and parallel stream of activities and roles that is totally
independent of the National Health Service. This is very different to
the situation in most other countries including the United States
where qualified counselling psychologists at tertiary institutions offer
a range of interventions from career counselling to brief therapy.

Watts and Esbroeck (1998) see the new concept of career as 'the
individual's self-managed progression in learning and in work'. They
identify two major antecedents for this. First, higher education guidance and counselling services are called upon 'to prepare a much
wider range of young people for a much more flexible and turbu-
lent working world; and second . . . it needs to be part of a lifelong
learning system, accessible not only to young people but to individuals throughout life' (Watts and Esbroeck 1998: 89). According to
Watts and Esbroeck (1998: 90) guidance across all three personal,
educational and vocational arenas ought to be brought under one
umbrella to respond 'to the greatest diversity in the student population; strengthening the European dimension in guidance provision;
using new technologies; coping with the increased numbers in higher
education; and moving towards a more holistic approach to student
development'. From what we have seen, this is still probably a
statement of intention rather than a description of what actually
happens in most countries within the European Union.

Increasingly with the development of the Internet, and the new
rapid communication technology, there will be less need for careers
services at all levels to be mainly providers of information. They
need to focus more on helping individuals to select and process
information and train them to be 'active rather than passive in the
way they use it' (Watts and Esbroeck 1998: 95). The various roles
and services that the authors advocate should subscribe to their
'student-centred holistic model', and not 'seek to impose a particular structure, but rather to maximise the linkages within whatever
structure is adopted' (1998: 97). These 'linkages' could be at various
levels identified as

1 communication;
2 coordination;
3 cross-fertilization; and
4 integration.

They report examples of effective linkages in Austria, Germany
and Denmark, but the authors conclude, albeit with a hint of
condescension:

Changes in the labour market and other factors mean that guidance counsellors are faced with increasingly complex questions which often touch upon all three areas of guidance ... Moreover, the move evident in some countries away from addressing 'problems', towards a more developmental approach designed to develop autonomous individuals who are more able to cope with issues on their own, provides a basis for services to come together in relation to such development programmes, while still retaining distinctive specialisms for use as required in specific situations'.

(Watts and Esbroeck 1998: 98)

PARENTS AND GUARDIANS

Since 1997/98 careers services are required to prepare reports for the parents or guardians of pupils aged 15–16 years informing them of careers guidance provided to their children. They are also required to offer parents the option of discussing the report with careers advisers. Most DfEE briefing documents imply that the careers services should take responsibility in three areas, of informing, encouraging, and enabling parents and guardians in the career decisions of their young clients.

Contact with parents may be by telephone, or by use of local media including radio and newspaper articles and advertisements. Cost concerns may limit postal contact to what is known as 'pupil post' – sending literature via the son or daughter. This has not been found to be very reliable. Careers services also make use of school events attended by parents such as meetings of the PTA. Newsletters are another means of communicating with parents and guardians.

Careers services also mount careers fairs, presentation evenings, career exhibitions, parents' training courses, and open days at a careers centre. The open days or evenings are also extended to school governors, including parent governors. They also exhibit posters and static displays at community centres, libraries and other similar venues. Topics covered on workshops and seminars for parents include post-16 options, work experience, local labour market information, and the availability of temporary or part-time work. Some of these events may be mounted jointly with local further education colleges, employers and other training providers. The aim is often to challenge any stereotypical parental perceptions about post-16 opportunities.

TRADES UNIONS

Trades unions are increasingly expected to 'play a key role both as *advocates* and as *deliverers* of information, advice and guidance' (Ford and Watts 1998). They are expected to be providers of frontline guidance, although the term has a slightly different meaning to its use in higher education. It is frontline in the sense that it is possibly one of the very few pathways open to all 'economically active' adults in accessing professional careers guidance and counselling. It includes:

- *providing accurate information*, e.g. about opportunities, providers, and how to access more in-depth help;
- *signposting*, i.e. redirecting individuals to appropriate levels of advice and guidance within or outside the organization;
- *providing advice*, i.e. helping individuals to interpret information and decide on the most suitable course of action;
- *supporting and enabling*, e.g. in gaining the confidence to start and carry through a course of learning;
- *advocating*, i.e. negotiating directly with institutions or agencies on behalf of individuals or groups;
- *feeding back*, i.e. gathering and collating information on unmet, or inappropriately met, learning needs and encouraging providers to respond to these.

(Ford and Watts 1998: 2)

Unions are urged to draw on support from local networks of Training Enterprise Councils (TECs), colleges of further education, community education and local guidance providers including adult guidance services, and careers services to develop their competence for the task. A European Union-funded programme has initiated a Shop Steward Education and Training Adviser (SETA) project for union officers and representatives to 'enhance their awareness of educational advice and guidance, and to help them negotiate or provide front-line guidance for members' (Ford and Watts 1998: 5). It was partly funded by the Workers' Educational Association (WEA).

Other organizations with whom active collaboration need to be developed by agencies offering career guidance and counselling are 'Social Work departments, immigration, the probation service . . . the prison service' (Clayton 1999: 240), and agencies catering to homeless persons. There are around 15,000 local black and ethnic minority organizations in Britain that need to be consulted or kept informed of the services available to them. The Refugee Council's training and employment branch attempts to meet the career concerns of refugees, another group requiring a targeted approach.

YOUTH IN CUSTODY

That mainstream, blanket provision is not appropriate for most of the above groups is clearly revealed in a study undertaken with young people in custody (MacGregor 1999). To begin with, it has to be recognized that careers advisers have to be 'peripatetic, moving from wing to wing as required to meet clients who cannot move freely within the establishment' (MacGregor 1999: 25). Although overall far less time is available, careers advisers need more time with individual interviews because

> clients' options are less readily defined and the clients tend to have multiple needs . . . careers advisers spend on average less than half a day a week to serve client populations of up to 800 at any one time – up to 3500 throughout the year – compared to three and a half to four days a week spent within mainstream educational establishments.
>
> (MacGregor 1999: 25)

An abbreviated list of some of the specific concerns that make career counselling with youth in custody problematic, adapted from MacGregor (1999), is given below:

- Inmates are unaccustomed to face-to-face conversation.
- They are unaccustomed to the concept of careers guidance, many not having attended school for years or having truanted from school.
- Their standards of 'basic' social behaviour are such that they have 'difficulty even knowing how to sit properly during careers guidance interviews' (MacGregor 1998: 25).
- Their literacy and numeracy are at a very low level because many of them have been excluded or have truanted from school from an early age.
- They have difficulty relaxing and communicating freely with others.
- They may 'adopt the opposite approach and talk a lot but words do not reflect their true feelings and worries ("bluff and bravado")'.
- The adviser needs to comply with the Rehabilitation of Offenders Act.

Reviewing existing research and a review undertaken by the Chief Inspector of Prisons, MacGregor (1999: 26) concludes that it is necessary to have:

a holistic approach involving the expertise of different specialists . . . The most effective career advisers are those who work
as part of a team, collaborating with other specialists within
the establishment. Advisers working in an establishment
where the governor grades do not co-ordinate the agencies/
contractors or foster a spirit of collaboration inevitably feel
isolated and ineffectual.

The importance of non-formal guidance provision, and the support they need from professionals, for an effective, nationally available service, is highlighted in the scenarios developed in this chapter.
There is no denying that they are resource-intensive and even fra-
gile, in that they may not be replicated in a uniform way across
settings. They require delicate and sensitive interpersonal relationships developed over time for them to flourish. In short, policy
makers should take on board the need to develop a multidimensional,
well-resourced, counselling provision in careers guidance wherever
it is offered. It is highly likely that authorities fight shy of such
approaches since counselling outcomes may not be easily or immediately measured, and its provision standardized and replicated.

LABOUR MARKET INFORMATION (LMI)

It is government policy that labour market trends, patterns and
processes should inform the provision of careers education, guidance and counselling. It is not merely factual information about
labour market statistics that are expected to be presented, but more
importantly, information about learning opportunities.

Additionally, LMI produces what are called 'destinations data' in
the form of:

- the pathways and success rates of those who take particular routes–
  sometimes termed 'learning market information' or 'learning
  outcomes';
- the emphasis . . . upon the role of personal and transferable skills
  for employment, community and other activity as working patterns become more varied and the concept of career becomes
  more complex.

(DfEE 1998c: 17)

Careers services are required to report destinations data separately
for the Year 11, 12, and 13 cohorts of school pupils. The key partners with whom the careers companies need to work in order to

collect this information include; schools, sixth form colleges, further education and tertiary colleges, higher education institutions, Training and Enterprise Councils (TECs), training providers, Universities Central Council on Admissions (UCAS), local education authorities (LEAs) (education, grants and awards, social services), Benefits Agency, employers, voluntary bodies (e.g. special needs), neighbouring careers companies, parents and young people themselves.

In addition to the agencies listed above, careers companies liaise with 'a broad spectrum of other institutions and organisations . . . [which] make valuable use of destinations information' (La Court 1998: 10). They include post-16 strategic/policy forums, education business partnerships and compacts, chambers of commerce, regional government offices, further education and higher education funding councils, libraries, elected MPs and local councillors, and the local media.

The importance of this activity from the point of view of the government is emphasized by the following statement of the Parliamentary Under-Secretary of State for Education and Employment, the Hon. James Plaice MP:

> One of the key challenges at national, regional and local levels is to improve further the use of labour market information in putting together provision which meets individuals and employers' needs and contributes to the nation's competitiveness.
>
> (DfEE 1995)

Where counselling in careers guidance differs from most other types of counselling, or generic counselling, is that clients and others expect access to a wide-ranging information database through the careers adviser or counsellor. When destinations data are supplemented by other 'soft' information such as case studies it can enhance the relevance and credibility of the guidance and counselling process. Broadly speaking, LMI can be used to break down the traditional 'opportunity structure' stereotyping and raise young people's aspirations. As La Court (1998: 14) says:

> Destinations information can help towards giving the Advisor greater credibility with their clients because such information is derived from local survey-based work and is timely and relevant to . . . young people.
>
> [It] highlights areas where Careers Advisors may need to challenge or reinforce a client's decision making processes, e.g. where there is evidence of stereotypical choice or competitive demand.

It provides useful information to encourage disaffected young
people to make positive choices from the available options and
to counter misconceptions that there are no [real] jobs or that
training programmes don't lead to permanent employment.

NEW TECHNOLOGY

Increasingly, with the proliferation of information and communications technology, 'destinations data is [*sic*] also being incorporated in
interactive software [e.g. CD-ROMs] and on the Internet. Information technology (IT) offers enormous potential in this and other
areas of LMI, particularly with regard to use by young people who
generally find it appealing and easy to use' (La Court 1998: 15). In
a NICEC Briefing, Offer and Watts (1997: 1) begin by saying:

> The Internet could have massive implications for careers work.
> It has the potential to make careers information more accessible
> than ever before. It could also lead to new careers education
> and guidance practices.

Since the Internet is 'an unmediated link (except for the hard-
ware) between user and information provider' (Offer and Watts
1997: 3), users are free to follow their own path through what is
essentially a vast reservoir of 'unfiltered information'. Offer and
Watts (1997: 2) continue:

> In a careers context, this can increase the scope of their [cli-
> ents'] ideas about opportunities, encourage lateral thinking about
> what might be of interest, and appeal to those who see seren-
> dipity as an important part of career learning and development.

The authors believe that individual guidance and counselling
could be provided 'at a distance' using email coupled with video
conferencing if such facilities are made widely available 'by providing workstations in public access points, community centres or
telecottages' (Offer and Watts, undated: 3). Already email in the 'chat
mode' allows two email users to view the text sent and received
simultaneously. The two people thus engaged in conversation could
be a client and his or her careers counsellor. Evaluation of pilot
projects using IT in careers counselling have been conducted and
are discussed below.

JIIG-CAL Limited, the trading arm of the Careers Research Centre,
University of Edinburgh, 'put forward a proposal to the DfEE for a
systematic evaluation of three technological approaches to delivering

careers guidance at a distance, namely Video Conferencing, Audio Conferencing and Telephone' (Closs and Miller 1997: 8). The most important and relevant findings were that all three technologies 'can effectively deliver career guidance interviews', the success of which 'depended on the content of the guidance, not on the technology' (Closs and Miller 1997: 6). Video conferencing 'was found to be helpful in establishing rapport in the early stages of the interview' and was seen to be 'cost effective where advisers spend a lot of time travelling to conduct a small number of interviews' (Closs and Miller 1997: 7). If that is the case, cost effectiveness should be used to argue for the provision of more effective counselling in careers guidance, as against the ubiquitous and all-too-brief interview.

Another research project which 'investigated the influence of computer technology' in careers work in schools found 'no simple relationship between the computer support available in schools and the career preparedness of students' (Hall *et al.* 1998: 6). It is only when computer support is used as an adjunct to 'a structured careers education and guidance programme, [with] commitment by senior management and staff . . . and good relationships between schools and careers services', that 'students were judged to be best prepared' (Hall *et al.* 1998: 8). Here again counselling appears to be the optimum mode for working with students. Hall *et al.* (1998: 8) conclude:

> Students' use of computer support packages appear not to play a role in the guidance interviews and so to have little impact on them. The time available for interviews, together with access problems, constrains the use which careers advisers can make of computer support during the interview.

As pointed out earlier, if the cost factor is kept under control, video conferencing appears to be one of the better solutions to the problems as identified by Hall *et al.* (1998) above.

INDIVIDUAL LEARNING ACCOUNTS (ILAs)

Another government initiative is the University for Industry (UfI) linked with a national framework of Individual Learning Accounts (ILAs). The current Labour government (at the time of writing) pledged to 'launch 1 million ILAs subsidised via TEC resources. In return for a contribution of £25, 1 million individuals will receive a TEC contribution, most likely in the form of a credit, of £150' (Corney and Watts 1998). The ILA is based on two key principles:

that individuals are best placed to choose what and how they want to learn to improve their prospects in the world of work; and that the responsibility for this is best shared, in varying degrees, among employers, the state, and the individuals themselves.

Information, advice, and professional guidance are the three main strands of provision to be purchased with the ILA. As defined by Corney and Watts (1998), professional guidance is the strand that comes closest to the counselling element in careers guidance. It is instructive to reproduce all three working definitions of the DfEE sponsored NICEC/CRAC policy consultation adopted in association with the National Advisory Council for Careers and Educational Guidance:

Information refers to data on learning and work opportunities conveyed through printed matter, audio visual materials or computer software, or through information officers in careers services or helpline services such as Learning Direct.

Advice refers to providing an immediate response to the needs of clients requiring a more than straightforward information response. It is usually limited to helping with the interpretation of information and with meeting needs already clearly understood by the client, and may or may not include signposting to a guidance interview where a more in-depth response can be provided.

Professional guidance refers to an in-depth interview conducted by a trained adviser which helps clients to explore a range of options, to relate information to their own needs and circumstances, and to make decisions about their career – i.e. their progression in learning and/or work. It may or may not include psychometric assessment.

(Corney and Watts, undated: 2)

The training information and advice telephone helpline Learning Direct mentioned earlier, which is 'free and impartial to all members of the public' (DfEE, undated: 9), has been used by over 340,000 people in its first six months of operation. It is expected that when it is extended through the University of Industry, it could 'handle 1.5 million calls annually' (DfEE, undated: 3).

In its bid to improve the 'quality and coverage of local services' to adults the government aims to 'build upon the services that already exist and are known to local people' (DfEE, undated: 5). Counselling however, is not on the menu, except perhaps as 'a brief discussion with an adviser, whether face-to-face, on line or by telephone', with the mere hint of the possibility of 'a more detailed guidance interview' (DfEE, undated: 5) for those who need it.

CONSUMER COUNCILS

In addition to market research, and other methods of liaising and seeking feedback from users of careers counselling and guidance services, the use of consumer councils has also been a feature with some careers companies. Consumer councils differ from other methods mentioned, in that they are more or less 'standing groups' or committees formed by interested parties selected for a fixed period of time. However, a consumer group by itself could not be regarded as the only way or the best way of being 'in touch' with consumers or users of products and services. In addition to the user group or consumer panel (or council), other methods could include:

- complaints and suggestion boxes or procedures;
- listening to frontline staff;
- formal surveys (by post or telephone);
- focus groups (ad hoc, one-off).

Positive benefits of a consumer council or, preferentially termed 'user group' for the careers services are listed by Linda Williams (1996: 11) as:

- a way of enabling users to bring forward issues of interest and concern of which the organization may be unaware;
- a direct and relatively cheap way of talking to users to discover their views on existing products and services and to identify unmet needs;
- a way of exploring, in greater depth, issues raised through other methods of consulting customers (such as surveys, suggestions and complaints procedures);
- an early warning system for pre-empting complaints or problems;
- a means of testing out proposals for changes in products or services;
- an opportunity to have a dialogue with users and explore their views in greater depth than is possible by surveys;
- a forum for clarifying misunderstandings and avoiding conflict;
- a creative and practical means of exploring solutions to problems.

PARTNERSHIPS

Although falling within a national framework, the delivery of adult information, advice and guidance services is to be effected through local partnerships. This strategy is meant 'to avoid competition between different local agencies, where that detracts from the quality of service available to local people' (Williams 1996: 7). However, there have to be links with national organizations 'including in particular the Employment Service, Learning Direct and the University of Industry' (Williams 1996: 8).

Careers companies are statutorily required to enter into partnership agreements with educational institutions attended by their clients. Unlike with the old service level agreements, when the Careers Service was the responsibility of the local authority, emphasis is now placed much more on the shared responsibility between educational establishments and careers service providers. The DfEE, *Action Note 5* (1997a: 1) expounds the purpose of partnership agreements as follows:

> Partnership agreements are formal statements of working arrangements between careers services and schools/colleges (including Young Offenders' Institutions). They provide the opportunity to review jointly the effectiveness of careers education and guidance and to agree roles and responsibilities, resourcing, provision of information and other factors to ensure high quality careers education and guidance. Agreements should be reviewed and updated annually. They may also be reviewed more frequently and modified in response to changing needs and demands.

Although independent schools are not covered by the legislation, 'they may wish to adopt the provisions of the Act' (Education Act 1997). Research had shown that the best model of careers work between schools and careers services labelled the 'community guidance' model was one where the roles and responsibilities of careers advisers and carers, teachers or coordinators were carefully and closely integrated. Discussion and negotiation at senior level are recommended for both parties.

SUPERVISION

Bimrose and Wilden (1994), in a ground-breaking article, lament the marketplace mentality of the new careers service provision, which tends to accentuate the managerial aspects of supervision at the expense of professional and developmental roles. In their overview of the state of supervision in careers guidance they sketch the confusion in the use of the terms counselling, guidance, and careers guidance. While there is purportedly only one 'professional body –

the British Association of Counselling (BAC)', which regulates all counselling practice, guidance has four professional associations representing 'separate but related areas of guidance practice which do not share any initial or supervisory training' (Bimrose and Wilden 1994: 374, 375). The four are identified as the Institute of Career Guidance, the National Association of Careers and Guidance Teachers, the Association of Graduate Careers Advisory Services and the National Association for the Educational Guidance of Adults. These authors appear to subscribe to the notion of guidance as a generic term with counselling as one of five activities offered, the other four being informing, advising, teaching and feeding back.

However, the central importance of counselling in careers work is brought to light in their discussion of a conflict between management and practitioners due to the nature of funding arrangements tied to specific and measurable outcomes. When a pilot project which offered adults careers counselling highlighted the need for supervision and further training for practitioners,

> service managers organised a customised training course which led to accreditation ... However, the practitioners firmly rejected the proposal, requesting instead that the training they required ... should take the form of case-study discussions. Their rationale was clear. They wanted the opportunity to discuss difficult clients and needed this kind of supervisory support to enable them to decide how to work more effectively with their clients.
>
> (Bimrose and Wilden 1994: 379)

STANDARDS

In grappling with quality standards in careers education and guidance, the Qualifications and Curriculum Authority (QCA) has (understandably) concentrated on learning outcomes. The National Advisory Council for Careers and Educational Guidance has also produced a set of quality standards. While the aim of such standards is to ensure 'a national infrastructure of quality-assured services', Jackson and Haughton (1998: 5) give reasons as to why the application of standards to community or 'informal' guidance may be problematic:

- Guidance delivered through community settings is often provided as part of another service, making it difficult to apply a set of discrete, specific standards;

- The very nature of the provision means that the service is client-centred, often non-specific and not resourced in the same way as institutional careers guidance services might be – many of the Standards would not apply;
- Much of the structured guidance work provided through community settings is undertaken by the voluntary sector; budget and resource constraints will almost certainly inhibit compliance with the Quality Standards.

However, Jackson and Haughton at the end of their briefing 'based on feedback from a 24-hour NICEC/DfEE consultation with practitioners working in community settings' (1998: 1) recommend that one should:

acknowledge the value of the client-centred nature of community-based provision, and of informal and flexible access to a range of support activities to individual adults as crucial stepping-stones to learning or career development.

(1998: 6)

These authors have here unveiled the main reason why the authorities totally ignore counselling in careers guidance. Since outcomes are not easily measured it is difficult if not impossible to envisage uniform and agreed upon standards to encompass every eventuality. Bureaucrats need a rulebook of standards to apply within a clear framework of policy and guidance.

Nevertheless, there is now a freshly instituted Careers and Educational Guidance Accreditation Board (CEGAB 1999) charged with awarding a 'quality mark' for good practice in vocational and educational guidance. Both outcome and process oriented, the measures are obtained through 1) staff audit, 2) staff feedback, 3) client feedback, and 4) 'mystery shopper' reports. To qualify for government funding every agency that sets itself up to provide careers guidance and counselling should meet the criteria and gain the kitemark by the year 2001.

This chapter has explored a wide range of professional and partnership relationships that careers services as organizations and careers practitioners as individuals undertake, while noting that it is still in a process of flux and change. There is evidence of a great deal of government interest and policy making, coupled with uncertainty and confusion both conceptually and in practice at the coalface. Throughout this book a recurring theme has been the absence of an acknowledgement of the centrality of counselling to the whole enterprise of vocational or career(s) guidance. In spite of such an overt and, on reflection, a bizarre conspiracy of silence, there is ample evidence that many practitioners engage in, while some policy makers support (perhaps without complete awareness of what they mean or only as an atypical or marginal feature), a human activity without which developed societies could not have functioned effectively in the latter half of the twentieth century.

The lack of acknowledgement of counselling is addressed in Chapter 6, which is an analysis and a critique of the current status of counselling in careers guidance, with a prognostication of the trends underlying future directions for theory and practice in the twenty-first century.

· SIX ·

A critique of counselling in careers guidance

From what has been discussed so far, counselling in the context of careers guidance in the United Kingdom appears to have been an often unacknowledged activity to which only lip service had been paid by government authorities and policy makers. Contributing to this perhaps is the public misconception or misperception of counselling either as a response to a crisis, or with an attendant stigma attached (e.g. debt counselling), or even limited to an encounter with a pushy salesman (e.g. financial counselling). In any case, even professionally accredited generic counselling has yet to establish itself and gain credibility as a mainstream and valued occupation in Britain (Riddick *et al.* 1996; see below), much in contrast to other developed countries, especially the United States of America.

ON COUNSELLING IN CAREERS GUIDANCE

The development of the counselling concept in the United Kingdom repays examination. Daws (1976) asserts that we are 'too often ready to believe that the word counselling and therefore the activity for which it stands, is American'. According to Daws, clergymen in Britain had for a considerable time described their work as 'pastoral counselling' before the idea was 'reimported from America in the 60's' (1976: 3). He insists that although it was 'vocational guidance' that 'sired' counselling in its modern guise in Britain, it was 'mental health, aided by transatlantic obstetrics' that gave birth to counselling and was responsible for its nurture in Britain (1976: 13). In time, mental health claimed the infant all to itself. Daws laments the relegation of careers guidance to a minor place in counselling courses and the 'separation of "careers" from "counselling" in the minds of most teachers' and continues:

> The separation also has roots in educational history. Careers teaching (or rather, careers mastering or mistressing) has been with us for half a century unglamorous, Cinderella-like, lacking expectations of time, resources or training. By contrast, counselling is new, with it, prestigious, best kept for the 'difficult' cases and not wasted on simple careers work. It is defined by a year's training and leads to better paid posts of responsibility [and] very much more free time.
>
> (Daws 1976: 20)

In contrast, in the United States, almost since the beginning of the twentieth century the only kind of 'counselling' offered was in vocational guidance (Seligman 1996). The American National Vocational Guidance Association (NVGA) was established as far back as 1913, and in 1931 became the American Personnel and Guidance Association (APGA). The APGA boasted 42,000 members in 1984 as well as local and state divisions throughout the United States of America. In the 1990s membership had risen to over 50,000. Seligman (1996: 8) writes:

> APGA after years of debate changed its name to American Association for Counselling and Development (AACD), reflecting the altered and broadened role of the counsellor in the 1980s. In that same year [1984] the *Occupational Outlook Handbook* included listings for both general counsellors and mental health counsellors, providing for the national recognition of the establishment of the counselling profession. In 1992, the AACD assumed its current name to American Counseling Association (ACA) [with the] goal of parity with APA [psychology and psychiatry].

Humanistic counselling associated with the name of Carl Rogers became the 'third force' in the 1960s influencing the growth of the human potential movement. As a proactive and preventative intervention, not necessarily connected with the amelioration of pathology, it came to be recognized as a creative, life changing, positive force. Vocational counselling, later termed career counselling, began to draw upon this 'third force', distinguishing itself from psychoanalysis.

Meanwhile in the United Kingdom, Riddick *et al.* (1996) list eight areas or settings where counselling is offered, although the provision in some instances is likely to be patchy and uncertain. They are:

- counselling in medical settings;
- counselling at work;
- counselling in the community;
- counselling in pastoral care;
- counselling in schools;
- counselling in further education;
- counselling in higher education; and
- counselling in private practice.

Yet there is not the merest hint anywhere that counselling is offered or could be offered in careers guidance. In the authors' list, counselling at work refers more to personal counselling in the form of, for example, Employee Assistance Programmes, rather than counselling directly related to matters concerning employment. Some large organizations, which use assessment centres for selection, may use similar methods in the form of development centres to provide in-house career counselling, where psychometric tests, work samples, interviews and feedback and not counselling are the primary components of such interventions.

The chairman of the test publishers Oxford Psychologists Press Limited (McHenry 2000), introducing a new range of 'user-friendly' tests discusses the 'challenge of combining psychometric testing with new technologies such as the Internet'. He urges that even some traditional psychometric tests should not be treated as simply having

fixed attributes like validity and reliability. They communicate an experience: feelings, associations, memories. They are best introduced on the web only when it becomes capable of supporting interpersonal interaction and delivering a rich, experimental environment.

(McHenry 2000: 1)

It is unusual for a test publisher to acknowledge such intangibles as more important than the psychometric properties of his tests. The way to enhance quality of human interaction is through counselling.

Most careers guidance practitioners' lack of enthusiasm for counselling may be self-defeating in the new realities of a postindustrial, knowledge-based society (Wijers and Meijers 1996). Understanding and managing anxiety in careers guidance becomes ever more important since 'the occupation is undergoing the same fate as the church tower: both have lost their significance as landmarks' (Wijers and Meijers 1996: 189). Increasingly careers practitioners 'have to help people . . . deal with the losses of [an] expected future – no more jobs for life, nor the opportunities of one's parents' generation,

and . . . the consistent physical and social environment of the workplace' (Sonnenberg 1997: 469). The conclusion that Sonnenberg
comes to is typical of this general concern.

> Career counsellors, brought up with the expectation that they
> ought to give tangible and useful guidance to their clients, now
> have to face their own impotence in the face of the limited
> possibilities that may be on offer. The usual defence against the
> anxieties thus produced is to become even more concrete, urg-
> ing clients to more and more information gathering, interviews,
> researches, psychometric tests etc., when the more difficult but
> more appropriate task is to help clients deal with tolerating the
> 'not knowing'.
>
> (1997: 471)

Sonnenberg here reveals the shortcomings of well-qualified
careers practitioners albeit with only limited 'skills' training in counselling, who appear not to be aware of 'the way their own anxiety
or urgency sometimes hastens the pace of their work, resulting in
a premature offering of practical solutions before the client has
worked through the emotional consequences of disappointment, loss
or threat' (1997: 470). Even if the careers practitioner is aware,
organizational and policy constraints limit what can be offered, which
has been a theme running throughout this book.

The limitations of current practices in career counselling have
been exposed in other ways. For example, it has been averred that
career counselling operates from a shallow theoretical basis. It
ignores the demand side, solely concentrating on the supply side,
where the imperative is for the effective and optimum utilization
of manpower. From the point of view of economics, labour is a
commodity with unemployment seen as a market mechanism within
the price/profit system. The implications of this for career guidance
and counselling have never been made explicit (see Overs 1979:
13). Increasingly, market-economy principles are applied to the provision of careers guidance too as in other areas previously deemed
to be a social good and publicly funded.

While advocating 'Green Guidance' to counteract the excesses of
capitalism with its obsession for economic growth, Peter Plant (1999)
paints a picture of what it is to be a careers guidance practitioner
within the system.

> One of the major aims of guidance is to lubricate the education,
> the training, and the labour markets in order to create or sus-
> tain economic growth. The counsellor acts as a human capital

investment adviser: where will it pay to invest my training?
What sort of careers will pay off in the long run?

Much of the time the career guidance process is seen as a linear
continuum with information giving and advice at one end and
counselling at the other. Testing, feedback and advocacy may be
situated at some point between the extremes. Such linear models
are oversimplifications and we need to accept that there are aspects
to human thinking that are qualitatively different from information
processing.

NARRATIVE, COUNSELLING, AND THERAPY

Hans Eysenck's critique of psychoanalysis, and by implication all
other 'talking therapies' including counselling as 'an unidentified
technique applied to unidentified problems with unpredictable
outcome' (1961: 6), may not have damaged the reputation of counselling in Britain as completely as once thought. Public accountability,
however puts increasing pressure on those who hold the purse
strings to seek 'evidence-based' treatments. In spite of this, Eysenck's
recommendation for rigorous training for therapy now appears somewhat off the mark in the light of new paradigm shifts in psychology.
If early in the twentieth century psychoanalysis was interminable,
requiring inexhaustible funds, the new brief therapies including
behaviour therapy of the late twentieth century err on the side of
being the 'quick-fix' of a managed health care system. Criticism of
this state of affairs is even more damning.

> fast food approach to therapy . . . may be undermining the coher-
> ence of this society . . . Perhaps the reason therapy is costing so
> much, and psychopharmacology has become so popular over
> the years, is that people have simply stopped listening to the
> world around them . . . Not only have people lost their connec-
> tion with each other, but individuals have also lost their con-
> nection with the planet on which they dwell.
>
> (Bütz 1997: 198)

Contrary to this pessimistic view, other commentators in the United
States see counselling as a burgeoning field. 'People considering a
"helping profession" will find that the array of opportunities continues to expand' (Collison and Garfield 1996). These authors list at
least 10 counsellor positions so designated that have proliferated
during the 90s in the USA. At least three of them are directly

concerned with careers guidance and counselling. They are (in anglicized spelling):

• school counsellor;
• student affairs counsellor (higher education);
• careers counsellor and outplacement counsellor (business and industry);
• counsellors in private practice;
• employment counsellor (federal and state agencies);
• correction counsellor (prisons and penitentiaries);
• youth counsellor;
• vocational rehabilitation counsellor (social services, hospitals, university campuses, local school districts etc.);
• military education counsellor;
• rehabilitation counsellor (health).

The difference between this list and the list earlier in the chapter (from Riddick *et al.* 1996) is that the above are actual positions available to trained counsellors whereas in the UK we have seen how sparse and ill-paid such positions are. Indeed, organizations in statutory, voluntary, and even commercial sectors, appear to prefer the untrained volunteer to even a marginally more expensive paid counsellor.

More than ever, it is necessary for counselling to become a social process in which 'cultural norms and values of society are affirmed' operating 'as a means of helping individuals to negotiate their own relationship with these cultural norms' (McLeod 1999: 217). In counselling and therapy, increasingly one moves away from the concept of an autonomous, bounded, individual self, when 'the good life depends on relationship, communality, tradition and place' (McLeod 1999: 220). Counselling and therapy may not always result in a 'cure' or symptom resolution, but as McLeod insists: 'It is not a question of healing', but a way of bringing people together 'to take part in a human conversation that goes beyond any of us as individuals' (1999: 222).

McLeod begins his ground-breaking book, *Narrative and Psychotherapy* (1997: 2) by re-examining and redefining the field, also implicitly underlining why counselling and therapy do not take the same form and salience in different cultures and at different periods in time:

Psychotherapy and counselling must be seen as a cultural form. It is a culturally sanctioned form of healing (or correcting) that reflects the values and needs of the modern industrial world.

The telling of personal stories, tales of 'who I am', 'what I want to be', or 'what troubles me', to a listener or audience mandated by the culture to hear such stories, is an essential mechanism through which individual lives become and can remain aligned with collective realities.

Applied to career counselling, such a view takes on even more significance especially when the consensus is that effective counselling treats the whole person as opposed to maintaining distinctions between career and non-career domains. The social constructionist, narrative approach to career counselling is well illustrated in the following:

> What a counsellor must help sustain is a broader perspective of career in immediate courses of action, and this perspective is quite similar to narrative construction. For example, traits are scattered until integrated in a character. Character is groundless until placed in a plot. The narrative thrust of the plot defines situations, populates the world with character types, and clarifies direction. A narrative cannot be enacted without a proper setting, and so on. Narrative construction is an integrative form of interpretation that gives parts (a trait, an action) significance as contributions to a whole.
>
> (Cochran 1997: 122)

Since much of 'counselling psychology' is still practised within the old positivistic paradigm, most critics see it as a 'technology of subjectivity' which, to a large extent has become reified (Russell 1999). The concept of the bounded self has been central to western psychology from the beginning and was co-opted into counselling and psychotherapy. It is increasingly being criticized from within these disciplines. Janice Russell (1999: 351), having examined the 'social construction of self' concludes:

> Careers guidance [is] a social practice instrumental in the production of selfhood with little attention to the political and social context in which this occurs . . . Counselling propagates specific and individualist notions of selfhood, with full attention given to internal processes, yet little to an external context . . . It is questionable whether the values of such a movement are compatible with some of the paradoxes with which individuals must cope in a rapidly changing social order. [The author's] exhortation . . . is to a re-examination of the notion of selfhood with which counselling is reflexively involved.

Questions about the concept of self and identity arise when 'mainstream institutions fail to provide parameters and guidelines' in a globalizing postmodern world, which compel individuals to create identities 'from within' (Russell 1999: 346). However, as philosophers affirm, 'ontologically the individual and the collectivity are inseparable' (Jahoda 1986: 253). In attempting to connect to reality, the counsellor becomes the representative of the broader social world and his/her acceptance and availability to listen to clients' stories is the 'first indication to the person that what they wish to say could be acceptable to other people too' (McLeod 1999: 219). For McLeod, counselling is a 'feeling conversation', a dialogue through which painful or confused areas of experience can be discussed and becomes a means of reconnection and validation.

> Some counsellors are good at offering 'standardised' understandings (often in the form of little sermons or lectures), but as a client, unless the understanding is an understanding of *me*, capturing all or most of the nuances and contradictions within my personal story, then it will not help me to gain a sense of really belonging . . . It is when the client begins to tell more specific, concrete stories of events, stories that convey more of the dramatic quality of their lived experience, and leaves spaces for conversational responses, that the counsellor is more able to enter the story and to be involved in co-creating narrative.
>
> (McLeod 1999: 219, emphasis in the original)

The definitive answer to Eysenck and others who represent the old paradigm that aims to standardize and systematize psychotherapy and counselling, is McLeod's (1999: 219) riposte from a social constructionist world view:

> Theories of counselling are no longer regarded as maps or mirrors of reality, reflecting 'objective' or 'real' facts about human beings, but as language systems which exist to enable dialogue over problematic aspects of experience, and as narrative 'templates' which offer alternative ways of telling the story of a life.

This position is further buttressed by John Shotter's (1995) arguments for a dialogical psychology where we are asked to jettison our familiar ways of perceiving the world as static images or 'pictures' but to see reality as being constructed (a process) through open-ended dialogue without final closure.

> the trouble with studying living phenomena historically . . . is that they cannot be adequately characterized in pictures, or

any other merely spatial schemes . . . as temporally unfolding activities or events, at any instant in time, they are always, by their very nature, *incomplete*; their 'parts' (if we are justified in using such a thoroughly inadequate term) cannot by defini-tion, all be present at once . . . it is impossible for any living process to be 'pictured-at-an-instant'. For there is always more of such processes to come, a 'more' of a genuinely novel kind that cannot be captured in any context free set or system of rules and principles.

(Shotter 1995: 163)

Jerome Bruner (1986, 1987, 1990) has consistently advocated a parallel form of inquiry to the traditional, empirical approach to psychology, which he termed cultural psychology. He demonstrates that we understand others and ourselves by thinking in narratives, and that 'we *become* the autobiographical narratives by which we "tell about" our lives' (Bruner 1987: 15). He maintains that 'a life as lived is inseparable from a life as told' (1987: 31).

It was Theodore Sarbin, as editor of a collection of articles entitled *Narrative Psychology* (1986), who first introduced the concept of the narrative approach as a 'root metaphor'. Since then, social constructionist, discursive models of human behaviour have been gaining ground as root metaphors in psychology, psychotherapy and counselling.

McLeod (1997: 31) has recounted how the 'narrative turn' in psychology and social science 'gained pace and momentum in the 1970s and 1980s . . . Social scientists began to become aware of what was staring them in the face – that people structure experience through stories'. Kenyon and Randall (1997: 4) believe that the narrative perspective 'spread from academic psychology to psycho-therapy and psychoanalysis' with practitioners in all these discip-lines sensing that 'the essence of their work [was] a controlled process of storytelling, storylistening, and, as it were, story fixing'.

NARRATIVE APPROACH TO CAREERS COUNSELLING

As early as the 1960s Wrenn (1964) was advocating the position that careers counsellors should take a total, global view of their clients in their 'social/cultural predicament'. Hackett (1993) asserts that 'it is a false dichotomy to regard career counselling as separate from psychotherapy'. Herr (1997: 11) agrees that counsellors should not maintain 'overt distinctions between career and non-career domains', and argues that career counselling

may best be thought of as a continuum of intervention processes that range from facilitating self and occupational awareness, exploration of possibilities and the learning of career
planning skills, to stress reduction or anger management, issues
of indecisiveness, unemployment and work adjustment issues.

Rounds and Tracey (1990) propose that career counselling should
be seen as a subset of psychotherapy. Seligman (1994) insists that
'perspectives in career development have continued to expand and
become increasingly holistic'.

Today, people, places, things and ideas one encounters in a lifetime are, more than ever, likely to change. Most people are connected to the World Wide Web both at work and at leisure. The
world for them is demonstrably information rich but action poor.
It is therefore less and less important for careers counsellors to
be providers of direct information. Instead, they must help clients
develop skills to sift and manage this information overload. In
such a context, an interview with a departing chief executive of
the Institute of Career Guidance (ICG) reported in *Career Development International*, entitled 'Careers for the New Millenium' sounds
apocryphal. Cathy Bereznicki (Lloyd and Bereznicki 1998) sees career
guidance as either information giving, and, even more information
giving in the guise of guidance – or nothing. Apparently, the word
counselling is not in her vocabulary.

> Careers guidance works at [the] . . . individual portfolio level.
> Let me give you an illustration. Someone recently asked me
> the best driving route back to London from a Midlands town.
> At the information level, I could have given him a map and
> perhaps the phone number of the RAC. I could have offered
> advice on the routes themselves in terms of mileage, distances
> between service stations, likelihood of traffic hold-ups etc. If I
> was [*sic*] to offer guidance I would have needed to know about
> his preferred style of driving, the capacity of the car he was
> using, whether he preferred motorways to other roads, how
> long he could drive before taking a rest, whether he had par-
> ticular dietary needs, whether there was a deadline for him to
> reach his destination. It would have been much more personal
> and would have helped him choose a route well matched to his
> needs.
>
> (Lloyd and Bereznicki 1998: 268)

Without taking a counselling stance, minimally defined here as 'a
change-oriented process that occurs in a contractual, empowering

and empathetic professional relationship', how would Cathy
Bereznicki know that the information she is giving as guidance,
even after direct questioning, is what the client really needs and
wants? The inevitably selective and biased nature of the information database available to the guidance provider is clear. The whole
business is entirely adviser-centred. It is a fact though, that careers
advisers, most of whom are members of the ICG, when performing
a statutory role, do not have even this much time to devote to the
average client. In the new millennium, an interactive computer
programme would offer far more careers information than Bereznicki
and her ICG members could offer at much lower cost and far less
inconvenience. In career terms, there will be very few fixed destinations to which there are known routes, and counsellors and clients will have to become joint explorers of unknown continents
through unfamiliar terrain. According to Audrey Collin (1996b)
practitioners of career guidance can no longer remain map-readers
or even map makers, but must emulate cooperative and creative
improvisers – for example, jazz players.

Cochran (1997) believes that the main task of career counselling
is to help people construct and enact more meaningful career narratives. He describes the enterprise of career counselling as a manifesta-
tion of the Aristotelian concept of practical wisdom. It helps people
'tell richer, more continuous, coherent, plausible, and productive stories' (1997: 24). As with all social constructionists Cochran
believes in human agency; 'the propensity . . . to be a causal agent,
actively producing desirable changes in situations', where 'an immediate aim of career counselling is to strengthen action' (1997: 119,
26). He does not find the systematic, step-by-step approach to career
counselling as depicted and idealized for example, in DfEE literature,
particularly useful.

> steps are not formed to reflect the reality of lived experi-
> ence . . . The lived experience is a dialectic of self and career,
> that is not given to step description. There is for instance,
> no special time to gather information, evaluate, form a portrait,
> explore options, or choose. All of these ingredients are present
> throughout counselling.
>
> (Cochran 1997: 41)

Very few careers, as we have seen, are 'linear and orderly', they
are increasingly 'negotiated and contingent' (Collin 1996a: 19). Collin
expects the career counsellor to be aware of the current changes
where tasks, jobs, and work are being released from the long held
'conceptual occupational structure' to be located anew 'in the

negotiated and shifting realities of organizational life' (1996a: 3). For her, the new 'career results from the interaction not only between individual and individual, and individual and organization but also between organization and environment' (1996a: 13). Recent vacancies for positions as Webmasters are a good example. Although the individual strives to be an 'agent' in Cochran's world view, Collin cautions against considering the person as a discrete and autonomous *natural entity*, reminding us of the discussion of 'self' earlier. She exhorts 'career psychology [to] reconceptualize career to incorporate a recognition of the role of organizations in it, and, more fundamentally [the organization's role] in the construction of the individual' (1996a: 2).

Kenyon and Randall (1997) confirm the above, but from a slightly different perspective. They maintain that a career or life narrative is not supplied by the counsellor, but that it is 'a story-line that is "out there" in the culture', bringing with it 'different ways of acting in the world and different types of relationship with others' (1997: 137). By the same token, 'a projected career cannot be . . . defined [only] by tasks . . . an occupation changes over time, making it difficult to specify tasks . . . A narrative of the future gives form to a career while leaving much that is open or indefinite' (Cochran 1997: 31). In such a scenario, providing specific information is likely to be partial, or soon to become out of date, and would therefore have only a limited function in the hands of future careers advisers and counsellors.

Cochran (1997) does not necessarily fully subscribe to the social constructionist ethos when he argues for the narrativization of individual careers as a special case and as a self-invested future representation. For example, he distinguishes the work of the economist from that of the concerns of a career counsellor's clients, as more objective.

> [We] expect an economist to make economic projections based on an objective body of knowledge and evidence. We would not expect them to be based on preferences, interests, likes and dislikes, personal values and . . . his or her personal orientation to living. For a representation of one's own future, however, personal orientation would be dominant, whereas objective information would be secondary and supportive.
>
> (Cochran 1997: 2)

This however, is not the last word. Scholes and Morton, two economists who won the Nobel Prize in 1997, generated an exact mathematical formula to take the guesswork out of derivatives trading in the stock market and make it a 'precise discipline'. The traditional dealers who used hunches, intuition, tacit knowledge and their life-narratives to position themselves in the market were dismissed as operating unscientifically, and maintaining their domin-ance in the market through sheer luck. The TV critic in *The Sunday Times Culture* magazine (2 December 1999), reporting on the BBC2 *Horizon* programme (*The Midas Formula*) on the ensuing debacle, concluded:

> As if acting out some moral parable of greed and hubris, the two academics then joined forces with Wall Street dealers, form-ing a super-company designed to exploit their discovery. As they viewed the formula as foolproof, they felt free to trade and borrow on a spectacular scale. But the company went bust, and its collapse almost wrecked the global economic system.

So much for scientific objectivity! The two distinguished econom-ists had not taken into account, and could not have foreseen the metaphorical beatings of butterfly wings of chaos theory, in another corner of the planet Earth. Their 'super-company' had to be baled out by the US federal government. To a certain extent, Cochran returns to a social constructionist position when he asks rhetoric-ally; 'Within career counselling why is forming a logical argu-ment secondary to composing a good story?' (1997: 58). When the numerically conceptualized stock market does not always behave with mathematical precision, even Nobel prizewinning higher mathematics could not be applied to career counselling to make it more objective and scientific.

The careers counsellor working from the narrative perspective helps people to become aware of the structures they have built up through previous experience, learning and conditioning. The more people are able to do this the more they are able to 'influence their own subsequent development by the choices they make' (Cochran 1997: 91). Much less like the careers adviser of the future that Cathy Bereznicki envisaged, Cochran's career counsellor first has to secure agreement with the client and consolidate a therapeutic working alliance.

> A working alliance includes agreement on a purpose, agreement on means, and a warm bond of relationship. Agreement on purpose is a fundamental basis of cooperation . . . Agreement on means inspires hope and confidence, a sense of optimism that is crucial for an undertaking. And a warm bond establishes an atmosphere of caring. Caring is not necessarily or even desirably

sentimental nor given to sentimental displays. Caring indicates that the person, the problem, and what happens matter.

(1997: 42–3)

'HOPES AND AMBITIONS' FOR CAREERS COUNSELLING

Hemmed in by rules and bureaucratic procedures, and constrained by ever dwindling and time-bound resources while accountable to funding sources for measurable outcomes, it is difficult to see how the Careers Services of the United Kingdom could become prescriptively caring, let alone establish counselling relationships with all their clients. Among measurable outcomes which the DfEE require of the Careers Services are destinations data, but more often than not they are action plans hastily agreed under pressure to arrive at a tangible result.

Take the very real case of Charlotte (not her real name). Having explored at length Charlotte's career decisions, which changed several times over many years after secondary school, Hodkinson and Bloomer (1999: 19) say: 'To have helped Charlotte, we believe guidance would have to have been rather different from that implied in current Action Plans. It would have had to be exploratory, helping her to understand her own conflicting hopes and ambitions'. However, no one could undertake such exploration without the allocation of time and resources to career counselling, instead of simply offering careers advice and guidance, as the Careers Service is presently constituted. Hodkinson and Bloomer do smuggle in the concept of counselling without prior warning when they introduce the word for the first and only time, after discussing how Charlotte's 'conflicting hopes and ambitions' could have been 'addressed'.

> Such counselling would have had to focus on helping Charlotte understand her changing self. It should probably have been largely undirected, gently widening her horizons for action by helping her to see and evaluate alternative avenues, including those concerning employment.

(1999: 19)

It is quite clear that the authors are demanding career counselling in the narrative mode without perhaps even being aware of it. Reluctant to press the case for counselling they merely end their paper with the open-ended plea of:

Finally, we need to think more deeply about what the nature
of an appropriate guidance approach would be. In an age where
lifelong learning is a central plank in government policy, new
thinking around such questions is urgent.

(Hodkinson and Bloomer 1999: 19)

Hodkinson and Bloomer began their paper identifying some of
the policy constraints against Britain developing 'an appropriate
guidance approach'. They cite the Audit Commission and other
HMSO publications to support the claim that: 'For both Government
and Opposition, post-compulsory education and training policies
are based on a linear trajectory model of progression from education to employment' (1999: 15).

careers guidance policies are driven by the assumption that it is
desirable and possible for people to make clear, enduring decisions about their educational and occupational futures. Any
subsequent major changes of educational or training pathways
are assumed to be dysfunctional – the result of an unfortunate
accident, poor educational provision or guidance failure.

(Audit Commission 1993: 15)

In such a context, Cochran's (1997: 118) view that even occa-
sionally, the outcome of career counselling may not necessarily be
the choice of a job but 'a sense of adventure, of extension, of
challenge, or of expanding meaning', might be met with total incom-
prehension by the British authorities. They may not know what
to make of his insistence that the 'two main criteria for [career]
choice are anticipated enjoyment or involvement and anticipated
meaning and worth' (1997: 120). Cochran (1997: 19) sees career
decisions as 'a consolidation of personal identity, increasing one's
capacity to identify with narratives of the future'. He goes on to say
that a careers counsellor and client 'are like coauthors of a dramatic
script, and the parts of the script must fit' (1997: 95). For Cochran
(1997: 11), a career decision:

emplots a person as the main character in a life-defining story.
Career decision is a movement from being a spectator on one's
life (or some aspect of it) to entering within a drama that is life-
defining in whole or in part . . . In short, career decision is a
dramatization of one's course of life in work.

Cochran does not ignore entirely the opportunity structure model
of career decisions that continues to influence British thinking when

he says that career 'counselling is largely a negotiation of stories, both from the individual's life and from the ecological context' (1997: 134). He also allows for 'an ideal narrative and optional narratives [to] change over time. They are not fully formed, but forming as one goes along . . . the ideal and the possible are interdependent. One must adjust the ideal to what is possible and the possible to what is ideally desirable' (1997: 13). Cochran's experience is not that there is an 'absence of narrative, but rather a variety of narratives that might be inconsistent with one another, incomplete, or distorted. The role of the counsellor is to help adjudicate plots as if one were co-author of a story in the making' (1997: 139).

Cochran postulates four phases in constructing a narrative of the future. In the first phase, one engages in self-study, attempting 'to weave together, in a whole composition, the person's most fundamental motives, outstanding strengths, and salient interests and values' (1997: 84). In the second phase, one sets goals and plans. Goals and plans are ways to translate motives into viable possibilities for actualization. The goal of an agent is anchored in meaningful motives and challenges. In the third phase, one deliberately acts to reach a goal, monitoring progress and adapting to circumstances as required. In the last phase, one reflects on the action or actions, emphasizing and taking responsibility for what was done and how it all turned out. Further action may be taken in iterative fashion until goals are reached or new goals set.

A EUROPEAN RESPONSE

In the early 1990s, Glenys Watt (1996) was commissioned by the European Foundation for the Improvement of Living and Working Conditions to undertake action research on adult guidance and employment counselling in the member states. She found that long-term, persistent and pervasive unemployment due to rapidly changing labour market conditions was met with very different ad hoc responses from different EU countries. Watt found a 'complexity of provision' not always transparent to the users, but highlighted the 'increasing importance of counselling services as an integral element of active labour market services, particularly in relation to the long-term unemployed' (1996: 143). She singles out Denmark as having instituted progressive measures.

In her 'Summary of Recommendations' she emphasizes the need for counselling:

- people of working age will have a greater need for counselling services as they face this increased flexibility on the labour market with the more frequent job changes and altered career directions which it is likely to entail;
- the counselling services which are provided will require to be of high quality in order to meet the increasingly complex demands of users as they deal with this more flexible labour market;
- counselling services will be needed throughout a person's working life, particularly in periods of unemployment but also to prevent unemployment in handling transitions from one job to another more successfully and in seeking the appropriate skills to meet the demands of the changing labour market;
- the trend for counselling services to be offered on the open market is likely to continue and will itself have a number of implications, particularly in relation to the reinsertion of those who are marginalised within societies.

(Watt 1996: 144)

The last observation stems from the fear that 'as more counselling services are provided on the market, requiring the user to pay for them, the very people who are most in need of such services may find themselves excluded from them' (1996: 145). Watt's most specific recommendations for counselling are given under the heading 'Suggested Minimum Standards' (1996: 149):

Every unemployed person should have access to at least one hour of counselling regarding their future work/training/ educational direction on first learning that they are to be made redundant/on first becoming unemployed.

After this initial contact, unemployed people who fall into high risk categories . . . should be able to access, on a voluntary basis, a further two hours of counselling assistance at any point in the first six months that they are unemployed. Access to training programmes for this high risk category should be available from three months onwards.

After six months all unemployed people should complete a full Personal Development Plan with the assistance of a qualified counselling practitioner (up to three hours of counselling assistance). This should be on a voluntary basis.

After 12 months an intensive three day counselling and motivation programme should be offered. Preferably this should be voluntary.

After 24 months a compulsory one week's counselling and confidence building sessions should be provided.

REAL LIFE ILLUSTRATIONS

The Royal British Legion Industries' Vocational Assessment Centre was established in 1996 to help the transition of ex-servicemen and women, especially those with a disability, into suitable civilian careers. The facility is situated within the Royal British Legion Village in Kent where clients can be housed in self-contained single accommodation for the duration of the period of career counselling, which usually takes up to three days. Staffed by occupational psychologists, psychometric testing has, inevitably, been a feature since its inception. However, a simplistic model of 'test and tell' could not have worked, and I, as the senior occupational psychologist, decided to introduce a relaxed, storytelling and story-listening mode of career counselling appropriate to the client group. Testing continues, but as a secondary, tailored intervention agreed with the client and not imposed as a blanket measure. The use of the Measure of Guidance Impact (MGI) (Christophers *et al.* 1993) revealed, with only very few exceptions, that this mode of career counselling works (Jayasinghe and O'Gorman 1998).

By and large, service personnel, especially those below commissioned rank, are socialized from early youth into a way of life far more demanding in some ways, but cosseted and cocooned in others, than the rest of us. Unless one listens and gains some understanding of the forces and circumstances that have shaped such individuals, a return to Civvy Street, often less ordered and hierarchical than what they are used to, becomes problematical. The counselling process helps them understand civilian work life demands as somewhat different to service life, especially in the new contract and portfolio work culture. Even a comprehensive battery of psychometric tests and work samples will not elicit a single useable fact unless the counsellor relates to the client as someone with no other agenda than to disinterestedly help them achieve their own goals in a world of work that is changing fast.

Our clients find the transition to civilian life doubly difficult due to a whole range of disabilities that handicap them in the labour market. However, almost without exception, they display well above average levels of innate ability, or 'fluid' intelligence, even when they have left secondary school with few formal qualifications. Some have trades qualifications, which are often restricted to service occupations that have no equivalents in the civilian workplace. Family and social background are powerful influences on their choice of service career. A representative, composite case study is given below.

Tom, an Army Corporal aged 32, had passed his eleven-plus as a school-boy in the Midlands. He had not taken up the offer to attend grammar school as he preferred to be with his 'mates' and social equals at the local comprehensive. He preferred not to be an object of derision of either the 'snobs' at grammar school or his 'gang' from primary school. His grandfather whom he admired had served in the Army during the Second World War. He left school without qualifications before he reached the compulsory school-leaving age and enrolled as an Army Cadet. At 17 he joined the regular Army in one of the Infantry Regiments. He had served on tours of duty in Germany, Northern Ireland and in the Gulf, and had been awarded the appropriate medals. Although he had intended to remain in the Army for the full length of 22 years before retirement, he was now being medically discharged following an accident in the sporting field. He had been a good regimental athlete, basketball player and swimmer, winning several trophies. The injury was to his back and had become degenerative. He walked with a slight limp and with the aid of a walking stick. He was married with one child. Although he was presently living in married quarters, he would need to decide where to live once discharged.

On an intelligence test Tom's performance was at the top 2 per cent compared with population norms. He also had high scores on all aptitude tests ranging from Language Usage to Mechanical Reasoning. He did not appear to be surprised by the test results. His sole concern was to find a job – any job that would enable him to obtain a mortgage to buy a house if possible, or else, rent. His wife might be able to work part time, most likely in a supermarket in a role in which she had engaged before marriage. He did not see how he could afford to spend more than a few weeks in training for a civilian job. He had no idea what he could or wanted to do and reiterated that all he was trained to be was an infantry soldier.

An outgoing, relaxed person, who was socially at ease, further discussion revealed that during his service period Tom had volunteered for help in the Junior NCOs' mess. He had kept accounts and organized celebratory events and parties for service families. He did not think any of this was relevant but was prepared to talk because it was in his nature to be sociable. Besides, nobody in the military hierarchy or medical practitioners and specialists had much time to engage him in conversation. They appeared to be interested only in presenting facts from their point of view and as quickly as possible. He was surprised that I was prepared to talk about my own background in a uniformed service and my late entry into higher education along with the financial struggles it entailed. Through counselling he began to appreciate that he possessed skills other than soldiering and that he needed to acquire other job-specific skills if he was to make a satisfactory entry into the civilian job market.

On the second day of his assessment, he told me that he had thought a great deal about his situation, having glanced through a variety of published material available at the centre. He had seen advertisements for vacancies in leisure management. He felt that he could combine his sporting interests and his supervisory experience in managing a sports centre although he could no longer actively pursue sports or take up physically demanding work. He accessed the Course Discover computerized information database and found an Open College training course in leisure management that he could undertake in his own time studying at home. He also found that once he had decided where he was going to live, he could attend the local further education college to acquire National Vocational Qualifications (NVQ) at least up to Level 3 initially.

By the third day, Tom was confident that he was on the right track. He also decided to acquire competence in using a personal computer by following a five-day computer literacy and information technology (CLAIT) course at the Royal British Legion Training Company, Tidworth College. This was a residential course and would be funded by his regiment as part of his resettlement package. He was then provided with information on how to prepare a curriculum vitae. Drawing upon all that he had learnt about himself on the previous two days, and based on a specimen or template of a one-page c.v., Tom accomplished this with minimal help from the staff. He later admitted that he had paid someone to do a 'professional' c.v. for him which ran to three pages, but felt that it made general statements that he was unlikely to be able to defend at a job interview. Tom now had a feasible continuation to his narrative as a soldier in transition to a comfortable civilian work role. He was also aware that a job was not for life and that he would need to continue to upgrade skills to remain employable.

How lack of time and awareness of the need for counselling prevented a statutory resource in adult career guidance from providing actionable advice to a client is my next story. A man I interviewed for an employability report for submission to court by a firm of solicitors in a personal injury case had suffered a back injury more than three years ago. He had worked as a carpenter building the Channel Tunnel and had earned good money. About two years ago he had wished to return to employment at some level and had registered at the local Jobcentre. Being disabled, he was seen by the Disability Employment Adviser and referred to the statutory Disability

Service, then known as the PACT team. The PACT psychologist had used a couple of tests including a work sample and told him that he could transfer his hand skills to work in a sedentary position requiring little carrying and lifting. He was recommended training at St Loyes College, Exeter (a residential college for the disabled) in electronic production.

When I saw the man two years later, he told me that he did not follow through with the recommendation. Unemployed and unable to provide for his family at the accustomed level, his wife had left him. While still registered as unemployed and drawing benefits, he had used great ingenuity in moving up to Nottingham, having signed up for a one-year full time further education course in music management. He told me that before he trained at a Skillcentre to become a carpenter, he had worked intermittently as a disc jockey. He was very much into pop music, personally knew a few well-known performers or bands and would enjoy the life of a 'roadie'. He completed the music management course with that in mind. What he was immediately planning to do was to organize both classical and popular music events in the borough where he lived, and was already getting promises of sponsorship from the council and local commercial enterprises. This man was the protagonist of a totally different life story to that which the careers adviser had planned for him. Even though the admission of potential high earnings may have been prejudicial to his case for compensation of loss of earnings as a carpenter, it did not take me much time to elicit information on matters of far-reaching importance to him. He needed to be understood and listened to more than he needed to be financially compensated. Ordinary people are more resourceful than professionals are when it comes to their future well being.

EQUAL OPPORTUNITIES

Equality of opportunity is increasingly of importance in the information-based, globalized economy, with relative affluence within sight of most people in the developed world. Acquisition of knowledge and its use in the creation of prosperity should be open to all those who seek it. As Powell (1999: 22) argues:

Liberty, equality of opportunity and prosperity are mutually reinforcing. In fact, the greater the equality of opportunity, the greater the liberty in society, which lies at the root of cultural empowerment. In postmodern conditions a maximalist approach to equality of opportunity is arguably both essential and desirable.

When counselling ethnic minorities, the disabled and women, or other members of groups in danger of being marginalized at work, it is well to remember the power imbalances that still distort the career aspirations of most of them. It is imperative that counsellors listen before they intervene. They must remind themselves that:

> There is implicit power in 'authoring', in having a voice. Being powerful requires a willingness of other people to listen, to hear, to be influenced by what that voice has to say. There are many people in the world who possess little power of this kind, who are effectively 'silenced'.
>
> (Kenyon and Randall 1997: 93)

They go on to explain:

> Authoring in this sense . . . is more like a conversation, a process of finding further horizons of meaning each time the tale is told. To 'author' is to participate in narration, to construct meaning through storytelling.
>
> (Kenyon and Randall 1997: 94)

Women, having identified themselves to have been living within the frameworks, cultural precepts and stories told by men, are now some way towards finding their own voice. Ethnic minorities are continuing the struggle. Other minorities like the disabled, homosexuals and older workers have only just begun to enter into the dialogue, with some tangible gains already visible. Cochran (1997: 38) gives specific and clear instructions in how to engage the client in a joint exploration of career and related issues:

> Normal expressions of an effort to understand, such as comment, paraphrase, clarification, request for more information, and the like [are] sufficient. If the client is oriented, recruited to be a partner in exploring the nature of the problem as a foundation for planning what to do, the elaboration of a career problem is apt to flow smoothly.

Client-centredness does not mean the counsellor abdicating responsibility. Here again, Cochran's (1997: 64) advice is thoroughly practical:

> a more active role is desirable in which a counsellor makes corrections, challenges evaluations, suggests other perspectives, validates, broadens viewpoint, establishes distinctions, and helps fill out implications. Certainly, a counsellor must be judicious in being active. Impositions and a constant flow of disruptions

would be very undesirable. Nevertheless, in composing a life history, a counsellor is a co-constructor of meaning.

Career guidance practitioners are expected to be trained and be responsive to a host of cross-cultural, minority, disability, feminist and environmental issues within an ethical, human rights perspective.

CONCLUSION

In concluding this chapter and the book, it is instructive to report the result of a traditional investigation into the value of emotional expressiveness in job search, which underscores the argument presented here that the British practice of ignoring the centrality of counselling in careers guidance, is sorely mistaken.

> Spera *et al.* (1994) asked unemployed professionals to write about their thoughts and feelings surrounding their job loss, and found that those in an expressive writing group were twice as likely to find a new job within eight months than those in a control condition who had been instructed to write about their job plans but not to dwell on their feelings or opinions.
>
> (Kenyon and Randall 1997: 78)

This illustrates the fact that even if in a very small way, allowing people to voice their opinions and express their emotions empowers them to take control of their vocational future. Narrative career counselling would have enabled more of these professionals to return to a productive life whether in paid employment or in other ways. They needed to tell their story.

> Story is an ontological metaphor. We are the stories we like to tell. We tell stories to describe ourselves not only so others can understand who we are but also so we can understand ourselves. Knowing ourselves is inseparable from narrating ourselves (Schank 1990). 'Know' and 'narrate' may have the same etymological root (Mancusco and Sarbin 1983; Casey 1987).
>
> (Kenyon and Randall 1997: 39)

As Gergen (1999: 172) says, in the postmodern era, whether people continue to pursue careers or not, it is only counselling discourse that 'enables clients to *re-story* their lives, to conceptualize their life trajectories in new and more livable ways' (emphasis in the original). If the authorities and the wider public heed the warnings, careers guidance would cease to be the limited, subprofessional activity it is at present, but be incorporated as a major component of generic counselling.

It would then be no exaggeration to claim that, along with the Green Revolution, counselling, narrative, and dialogue may in the new millennium, ultimately prove to be the means of our survival in a habitable, sustainable planet.

Bibliography

Anderson, N. and Herriott, P. (eds) (1997) *International Handbook of Selection and Assessment*. Chichester: Wiley.

Argyle, M. (1989) *The Social Psychology of Work*, 2nd edn. Harmondsworth: Penguin.

Arnold, J. and Jackson, C. (1997) The new career: issues and challenges. *British Journal of Guidance and Counselling*, 25 (4): 427–33.

Audit Commission (1993) *Unfinished Business: Full Time Educational Courses for 16–19 Year Olds*. London: HMSO.

Bailey, D. (1987) Open learning and guidance. *British Journal of Guidance and Counselling*, 15 (3): 237–56.

Ball, B. (1984) *Careers Counselling in Practice*. London: Falmer Press.

Ball, B. (1987) Graduates and career guidance. *Guidance and Assessment Review*, Leicester: The BPS, 3 (3): 5–8.

Bandura, A. (1995) *Self-efficacy in Changing Societies*. Cambridge: Cambridge University Press.

Bedford, T. (1982) *Vocational Guidance Interviews Explained: A model and some training implications*. London: Department of Employment.

Benart, S. and Smith, P. (1998) *National Adult Learning Survey 1997: Summary*. Sudbury: DfEE and Social and Community Planning Research.

Bimrose, J. and Wilden, S. (1994) Supervision in careers guidance: empowerment or control? *British Journal of Guidance and Counselling*, 22 (3): 373–83.

Bordin, E.S. (1955) *Psychological Counseling*. New York: Appleton-Century-Crofts.

Bradley, S. (1990) The Careers Service: past, present and future. *British Journal of Guidance and Counselling*, 18 (2): 137–55.

Bruner, J. (1986) *Actual Minds, Possible Worlds*. Cambridge, MA: Harvard University Press.

Bruner, J. (1987) Life as narrative. *Social Research*, 54 (1): 11–32.

Bruner, J. (1990) *Acts of Meaning*. Cambridge, MA: Harvard University Press.

Butcher, V., Bell, E., Hurst, A. and Mortensen, R. (1998) *New Skills for New Futures: Higher Education Guidance and Counselling Services in the UK*. Cambridge: CRAC/NICEC.

Bütz, M.R. (1997) *Chaos and Complexity: Implications for Psychological Theory and Practice*. Washington DC: Taylor & Firmin.

CAMPAG (1998) *Mediation Standards: The National Organization for Education, Training and Standard Setting in Advice, Guidance, Advocacy, Counselling Guidance, Mediation and Psychotherapy*. Biggleswade: CAMPAG.

Career Guidance Today (1998) Stourbridge: Institute of Careers Guidance.

Careers and Educational Guidance Accreditation Board (CEGAB) (1991) www.guidance council.com

Casey, E. (1987) *Remembering; A Phenomenological Study*. Bloomington, IN: Indiana University Press.

Christophers, S., Stoney, S., Whetton, C., Lines, A. and Kendal, L. (1993) *Measure of Guidance Impact (MGI) Technical Manual*. Windsor: NFER/ASE.

Classification of Occupations and Dictionary of Occupational Titles (1972) Supplement (1982) London: Department of Employment.

Clayton, P.M. (1999) *Access to Vocational Guidance*. Glasgow: University of Glasgow.

Closs, S.J. and Miller, I.M. (1997) *IT in Guidance – An evaluation of Desktop Video Conferencing Technology*. Sudbury: DfEE.

Clutterbuck, D. and Hill, R. (1981) *The Remaking of Work; Changing Work Patterns and How to Capitalize on Them*. London: Grant McIntyre.

Cochran, L. (1997) *Career Counseling, A Narrative Approach*. Thousand Oaks, CA: Sage.

Collin, A. and Watts, A.G. (1996) The death and transfiguration of career – and of career guidance? *British Journal of Guidance and Counselling*, 24 (3): 385–98.

Collin, A. and Young, R.A. (1992) Constructing career through narrative and context: an interpretive perspective, in R. Young and A. Collin (eds) *Interpreting Career, Hermeneutical Studies of Lives in Context*. Westport, CT: Praeger.

Collin, A. (1996a) Integrating neglected issues into the re-conceptualization of career. Paper presented at the Symposium; The Birth and Death of Career: Counseling Psychology's Contributions, Toronto, 9–13 August.

Collin, A. (1996b) Re-thinking the relationship between theory and practice: practitioners as map readers, map-makers – or jazz players? *British Journal of Guidance and Counselling*, 24 (1): 67–81.

Collison, B.B. and Garfield, N.J. (1996) *Careers in Counseling and Human Services*, 2nd edn. Washington DC: Taylor & Francis.

Confederation of British Industry (1993) *Towards a Skills Revolution*. London: CBI.

Corney, M. and Watts, T. (1998) *Individual Learning Accounts, the Role of*

Information, Advice and Guidance, CRAC/NICEC Conference Briefing. Cambridge: CRAC.

CRAC/NICEC (1999) *The University for Industry and Local Information, Advice and Guidance Partnerships*, Conference Briefing. Cambridge: CRAC.

Crites, J.O. (1969) *Vocational Psychology, The Study of Vocational Behavior and Development*. New York: McGraw Hill.

Crites, J.O. (1981) *Career Counseling*. New York: McGraw-Hill.

Csikszentmihalyi, M. (1997) *Living Well, The Psychology of Everyday Life*. London: Weidenfield & Nicholson.

Davies, D. (1997) *Counselling in Psychological Services*. Buckingham: Open University Press.

Dawis, R.V. and Lofquist, L.H. (1984) *A Psychological Theory of Work Adjustment*. Minneapolis: University of Minnesota Press.

Daws, Peter (1976) *Early Days: A Personal Review of the Beginnings of Counselling in English Education during the Decade 1964–74*. Cambridge: Hobsons Press/CRAC.

Department for Education and Employment (DfEE) (1995) *Labour Market Information for Further Education Colleges – A Handbook for Practitioners*. Sudbury: DfEE.

Department for Education and Employment (DfEE) (1997a) *Action Note 5, Partnership Agreements*. Sudbury: DfEE.

Department for Education and Employment (DfEE) (1997b) *Better Choices, Key areas of professional development for careers co-ordinators in schools*. Sudbury: DfEE.

Department for Education and Employment (DfEE) (1997c) *Careers Education and Guidance in Schools*. Sudbury: DfEE.

Department for Education and Employment (DfEE) (1998a) *Action Note 6: Good Practice in Career Action Planning*. Sudbury: DfEE.

Department for Education and Employment (DfEE) (1998b) *Managing Change in the Careers Service*. Sudbury: DfEE.

Department for Education and Employment (DfEE) (1998c) *Taking Forward Careers Service Focusing, A Report on Five Regional Workshops*, Choice and Careers Division. Sudbury: DfEE.

Department for Education and Employment (DfEE) (1998d) *Talking about 'Careers': Young People's views of Careers Education and Guidance at School: Executive Summary*. November. Sudbury: DfEE.

Department for Education and Employment (DfEE) (1998e) *Teaching: High Status, High Standards: Requirements for Courses of Initial Teacher Training*, Circular 4/98. Sudbury: DfEE.

Department for Education and Employment (DfEE) (1998/1999) *Labour Market and Skill Trends*. Sudbury: DfEE.

Department for Education and Employment (DfEE) (undated) *The Learning Age: Local Information Advice and Guidance for Adults in England – Towards a National Framework*. Sudbury: DfEE.

Department for Education and Employment (DfEE) (2000) *Connexions: The Best Start in Life for Every Young Person*. Sudbury: DfEE.

Department of Education and Science (DES) (1973) Educational developments at home and abroad. A select list of recent additions to the library. DES Library No. 1 (April 1870) – No. 102 (October 1980). London: DES Library.

Department of Employment (1981) *The Careers Service and Employment: A Synopsis of Some Research Findings*. London: HMSO.

Dictionary of Occupational Titles (1991) revised edn. Indianapolis, IN: JIST Works, United States Department of Labor.

Earles, F.M. (1931) *Methods of Choosing a Career*. London: George G. Harrop & Co Ltd.

The Education Reform Act (1988) London: HMSO.

Erikson, E.H. (1950) *Childhood and Society*, 2nd edn. New York: Norton.

Evans, N. (1996) Letter in *Career Guidance Today*, 4 (1), 30.

Eysenck, H.J. (1961) Are there 'kinds' of counsellors? *Counselling News and Views*, 12: 5–9.

Farley, M. and Walsh, A. (1998) Freshstart. *Career Guidance Today*, 6 (2): 26–8.

Fielding, A.J. (undated) Where do we go from here? Constructing models of guidance for the millennium. *Occasional Papers in Career Guidance No. 2*. Stourbridge: Institute of Careers Guidance.

Ford, G. and Graham, B. (1994) The new qualification in careers guidance in higher education: a collaborative partnership. *British Journal of Guidance and Counselling*, 22 (1): 127–41.

Ford, G. (1998) *Youth Start Mentoring Action Project: The National and Local Impact of the MAP Project*. Stourbridge: ICG.

Ford, G. (1999) *Stepping Stones Project: Stage 1 Evaluation Report; Careers Guidance for Socially Excluded Young People*. Stourbridge: ICG.

Ford, G. and Watts, T. (1998) *Trade Unions and Lifelong Guidance*. Cambridge: NICEC/TUC.

Fryer, D. (1931) *The Measurement of Interests (in Relation to Human Adjustment)*. New York: Henry Holt & Co.

Gergen, K. (1999) *An Invitation to Social Construction*. London: Sage.

Ginzberg, E. (1958) *Human Resources, the Wealth of Nations*. New York: Simon and Schuster.

Ginzberg, E., Ginzberg, S.W., Axelrad, S. and Herma, J.L. (1951) *Occupational Choice: An Approach to a General Theory*. New York: Columbia.

Gottfredson, L.S. (1981) Circumscription and compromise. A developmental theory of occupational aspiration. *Journal of Counseling Psychology*, 28: 545–79.

Greenwood, A. (Forthcoming) *Workplace Counselling*. Buckingham: Open University Press.

Gysbers, N.C., Drier, Jr, H.N. and Moore, E.J. (1973) *Careers Guidance, Practice and Perspectives*. Worthington, OH: Charles A. Jones Publishing Co.

Gysbers, N.C., Heffner, M.J. and Johnston, J.A. (1998) *Career Counseling, Process, Issues, and Techniques*. Boston, MA: Allyn & Bacon.

Hackett, G. (1993) Career counseling and psychotherapy; False dichotomies and recommended remedies. *Journal of Career Development*, 1: 105–17.

Hall, J., Brown, C., Edwards, L. and MacLean, P. (1998) *IT in Guidance – Effective Use of Computers in Guidance*. Sudbury: DfEE.

Handy, C. (1984) *The Future of Work*. Oxford: Blackwell.

Hawthorn, R. (1996a) Careers work in further and adult education, in A.G. Watts, B. Law, J. Killeen, J.M. Kidd and R. Hawthorn (eds) *Rethinking Careers Education and Guidance*. London: Routledge.

Hawthorn, R. (1996a) Other sources of guidance on learning and work, in A.G. Watts, B. Law, J. Killeen, J.M. Kidd and R. Hawthorn (eds) *Rethinking Careers Education and Guidance*. London: Routledge.

Hawthorn, R. (1994) *The New Careers Service and Adult Guidance Strategies*, CRAC/NICEC Conference Briefing. Cambridge: CRAC.

Herr, E.L. (1989) Career development and mental health. *Journal of Career Development*, 16: 5–18.

Herr, E.L. (1994) Towards the convergence of career theory, mythology, issues and possibilities, in M.L. Savickas and B.W. Walsh (eds) *Handbook of Career Counseling, Theory and Practice*. Palo Alto, CA: Davis-Black Publishing.

Herr, E.L. (1997a) Career counselling: a process in process. *British Journal of Guidance and Counselling*, 25 (1): 81–93.

Herr, E.L. (1997b) Perspectives on career guidance and counseling in the 21st century. *Educational and Vocational Guidance*, 60: 1–15.

Hillage, J. (1994) *Measuring Satisfaction with the Careers Service*. Brighton: Institute of Manpower Studies.

Hirsh, W., Kidd, J. and Watts, A.G. (1998) *Constructs of Work Used in Career Guidance*, NICEC Briefing Paper.

Hodkinson, P. and Bloomer, M. (1999) Where 'right' is wrong. *Career Guidance Today*, 7 (2): 15–19.

Holdsworth, R. (1982) *Psychology of Careers*. Leicester: The BPS/Macmillan Press.

Holland, J.L. (1966) *The Psychology of Vocational Choice*. Walthan, MA: Blaisedell-Ginn.

Hollway, W. (1991) *Work Psychology and Organizational Behaviour: Managing the Individual at Work*. London: Sage.

Hopson, B. (1982) Counselling and helping, in R. Holdsworth (ed.) *Psychology of Careers*. Leicester: The BPS/Macmillan Press.

Hopson, B. and Hayes, J. (eds) (1968) *The Theory and Practice of Vocational Guidance, A Selection of Readings*. Oxford: Pergamon Press.

Hoyt, K.B. (1965) The Challenge of Guidance and Vocational Education. Address given at the 59th Annual Vocational Convention, Miami Beach, FL, December.

Hutton, W. (1995) *The State We're In*. London: Jonathan Cape.

Institute of Careers Guidance (ICG) (1996) *Career Guidance for Adults*. Stourbridge: ICG.

Institute of Careers Guidance (ICG) (undated a) *Career Guidance and Socially Excluded Young People: Working with Groups*, Briefing Paper. Stourbridge: ICG.

Institute of Careers Guidance (ICG) (undated b) *Lifelong Career Guidance for Lifelong Career Development*. Stourbridge: ICG.

Jackson, H. and Haughton, L. (1998) *Adult Guidance in Community Settings*. Cambridge: NICEC/CRAC/DfEE.

Jahoda, M. (1986) Small selves in small groups. *British Journal of Social Psychology*, 25: 253–4.

Jayasinghe, M. and O'Gorman, J.P. (1998) Vocational guidance of the disabled ex-service person at the Royal British Legion Industries. *The Occupational Psychologist*, No. 35: 22–7.

Jepsen, D.A. (1996) Relationship between developmental career counseling theory and practice, in M.L. Savickas and B.W. Walsh (eds) *Handbook of Career Counselling Theory and Practice*. Palo Alto, CA: Davis-Black Publishing.

Kelly, G.A. (1955) *The Psychology of Personal Constructs*. New York: Norton.

Kenyon, G.M. and Randall, W.L. (1997) *Restorying Our Lives; Personal Growth through Autobiographical Reflection*. Westport, CT: Praeger.

Kline, P. (1975) *Psychology of Vocational Guidance*. London: B.T. Batisford Ltd.

Krau, E. (1997) *The Realization of Life Aspirations through Vocational Choice*. Westport, CT: Praeger.

Krumboltz, J.D. (1993) Integrating career and personal counselling. *The Career Development Quarterly*, 42: 143–8.

Krumboltz, J.D. (1996) A learning theory of career counseling, in M.L. Savickas and B.W. Walsh (eds) *Handbook of Career Counseling Theory and Practice*. Palo Alto, CA: Davis-Black Publishing.

Krumboltz, J.D. and Thoresen, C.E. (1976) *Counseling Methods*. New York: Holt, Rinehart and Winston.

La Court, M.T. (1998) *The Use of Destinations Information by Careers Service Companies – A Survey of Current Practice and Issues*. Choice and Careers Division. London: DfEE.

Lang, P. (1999) Counselling, counselling skills and encouraging pupils to talk: clarifying and addressing confusion. *British Journal of Guidance and Counselling*, 27 (1): 23–33.

Law, B. (1981) Community interaction: A mid range focus for theories of career development in young people. *British Journal of Guidance and Counseling*, 9: 141–58.

Law, B. (1996) Careers work in schools, in A.G. Watts, B. Law, J. Killeen, J.M. Kidd and R. Hawthorn (eds) *Rethinking Careers Education and Guidance*. London: Routledge.

Law, B. (1999) Careers learning space; new DOTS thinking in careers education. *British Journal of Guidance and Counselling*, 27 (1): 35–54.

Lea, K. (ed.) (1997) *Cassell Careers Encyclopaedia*. London: Cassell.

Lloyd, B. and Bereznicki, C. (1998) Careers for the new millennium. *Career Development International*, 3 (6): 266–70.

Lunneborg, P.W. (1983) Career counseling techniques, in B.W. Walsh and S.H. Osipow (eds) *Handbook of Vocational Psychology, Vol. 2, Applications*. London: LEA.

Mabey, J. and Sorenson, B. (1995) *Counselling for Young People*. Buckingham: Open University Press.

MacGregor, F. (1999) Behind bars, careers service with 15 to 20 year olds in custody. *Career Guidance Today*, 1 (2): 373–83.

McHenry, R. (2000) Time for psychometric testing to move on? *OPPINIONS, The Newsletter for Oxford Psychologists Press Customers*, 17 January: 1.

McLeod, J. (1997) *Narrative and Psychotherapy*. London: Sage.

McLeod, J. (1999) Counselling as a social process. *The Journal of the British Association for Counselling*, August: 217–22.

Manusco, J. and Sarbin, T. (1983) The self narrative in the enactment of roles, in T. Sarbin and E. Schiebe (eds) *Studies in Social Identity*. New York: Praeger.

Morgan, C.T. and Hart, G.R. (1977) *Career Education in Australia*. Cambridge: CRAC/Hobsons Press.

Morris, M., Simkin, C. and Stoney, S. (1995) *The Role of the Careers Service in Careers Education and Guidance in Schools, Final Report*. London: NFER/QADU, Department for Education and Employment.

Munsterberg, H. (1913) *Psychology and Individual Efficiency*. Boston, MA: Houghton Mifflin.

Nelson-Jones, R. (1982) *The Theory and Practice of Counselling Psychology*. London: Holt, Rhinehart and Winston.

Newscheck (1999) Sheffield: Careers and Occupational Information Centre.

Newsom Report (1963) *Half Our Future*. London: HMSO.

Newton, T. (1997) Equality principles? Are we seriously bothered? *Career Guidance Today*, Institute of Careers Guidance, 5 (4): 27–30.

NICEC (1996) *How Career Decisions are Made*, Briefing Paper. Cambridge: NICEC.

NICEC/CRAC (1995) *Staff Development for Careers Work in Schools and Sixth-Form Colleges*, Briefing Paper. Cambridge: NICEC.

NICEC/ICG (1998) *Career Guidance Mentoring for Disengaged People*, Briefing Paper. Cambridge: NICEC.

Norris, H. (1999) Guidance for the millennium. *Newscheck*, 9 (9): 17–18.

Oakshott, M. (1996) The likely impact of introducing competence-based occupational standards in counselling/psychotherapy and guidance for learning in work. *British Journal of Guidance and Counselling*, 24 (1): 19–33.

Offer, M. and Watts, A.G. (1997) *The Internet and Careers Work*, Briefing Paper. Cambridge: NICEC.

Office for Standards in Education/Department for Education and Employment (Ofsted/DfEE) (1998) *National Survey of Careers Education and Guidance in Secondary Schools*. Sudbury: DfEE.

Overs, R.P. (1979) The interaction of vocational counselling with the economic system, in S.G. Weinrich (ed.) *Career Counseling; Theoretical and Practical Perspectives*. New York: McGraw-Hill.

Parsons, F. (1909) *Choosing a Vocation*. Boston, MA: Houghton-Mifflin.

Patterson, C.H. (1959) *Counseling and Psychotherapy*. New York: Harper.

Plant, P. (1999) Economy and ecology: towards Green Guidance. *International Careers Journal*, http://www.hexcentric.com/icj/jan99/cjap001s.htm

Powell, F. (1999) Adult education, cultural empowerment and social equality; the Cork Northside Education Initiative. *Widening Participation and Lifelong Learning*, 1 (1): 20–6.

Psathas, G. (1968) Toward a theory of occupational choice for women. *Sociology and Social Research*, 52 (2): 253–68.

Riddick, E., Hughes, C., Ross, R. and Whorral, H. (1996) *Guidance and Counselling*. Manchester: AGCAS/CSU.

Rivis, V. (1996) Symposium: Introduction: occupational standards for advice, guidance, counselling and psychotherapy, a critical review. *British Journal of Guidance and Counselling*, 2 (1): 5–8.

Robb, G. (1998) Survey of careers guidance OFSTED/DfEE. *Newscheck*, 9 (3): 3–4.

Roberts, K. (1968) The entry into employment: an approach towards a general theory. *The Sociological Review*, 16 (2).

Rodger, A. (1952) The seven point plan, in B. Hopson and J. Hayes (eds) *The Theory and Practice of Vocational Guidance, A Selection of Readings*. Oxford: Pergamon Press.

Roe, A. (1956) *Psychology of Occupations*. New York: John Wiley.

Rogers, C.R. (1951) *Client-Centered Therapy*. Boston, MA: Houghton-Mifflin.

Rose, R. (1983) *Getting by in Three Economies*. Glasgow: University of Strathclyde.

Rounds, J.B. and Tracey, T.J. (1990) From trait and factor to person–environment fit counseling. Theory and process (1–14), in W.B. Walsh and S.H. Osipow (eds) *Contemporary Topics in Vocational Psychology*. Hillsdale, NJ: LEA.

Rousseau, D.M. and Tinsley, C. (1997) Human resources are local: society and social contracts in a global economy, in N. Anderson and P. Herriott (eds) *International Handbook of Selection and Assessment*. Chichester: Wiley.

Russell, J. (1999) Counselling and the social construction of self. *British Journal of Guidance and Counselling*, 27 (3): 339–56.

Sarbin, T. (ed.) (1986) *Narrative Psychology, the Storied Nature of Human Conduct*. New York: Praeger.

Savickas, M.L. and Walsh, B.W. (eds) (1996) *Handbook of Career Counseling Theory and Practice*. Palo Alto, CA: Davis-Black Publishing.

Schank, R. (1990) *Tell Me a Story: A New Look at Real and Artificial Memory*. New York: Scribners.

Seligman, L. (1994) *Developmental Career Counseling and Assessment*, 2nd edn. London: Sage.

Seligman, L. (1996) *Diagnosis and Treatment Planning in Counseling*, 2nd edn. New York: Plenum Press.

Shephard, G. (1996) Good careers advice vital to a prosperous Britain – Shephard. *DfEE Press Release 67/96*, 4 March.

Shotter, J. (1995) In conversation: joint action, shared intentionality and ethics. *Theory and Psychology*, 5: 49–73.

Sievers, F.L. (1963) quoted in B. Hopson and J. Hayes (eds) *The Theory and Practice of Vocational Guidance, A Selection of Readings*. Oxford: Pergamon Press.

Sonnenberg, D. (1997) The 'new career' changes: understanding and managing anxiety. *British Journal of Guidance and Counselling*, 25 (4): 463–72.

Spera, S.P., Buhrfeind, E.D. and Pennebaker, J.W. (1994) Creative writing and coping with job loss. *Academy of Management Journal*, 37: 722–33.

Standard Occupational Classification, Vol. 2 (1995) London: HMSO.

Stoney, S., Ashby, P., Golden, S. and Lines, A. (1998) *Talking About Careers: Young People's Views of Careers Education and Guidance at School*. Sudbury: DfEE/The Careers Service.

Strong, E.K., Jr (1943) *The Vocational Interests of Men and Women*. Stanford, IND: Stanford University Press.

Super, D.E. (1957) *The Psychology of Careers*. New York: Harper and Row.

Super, D.E. (1980) A life-span, life-space approach to carer development. *Journal of Vocational Behavior*, 16: 282–98.

Super, D. (1983) The history and development of vocational psychology: A historical perspective, in W.B. Walsh and S.H. Osipow (eds) *Handbook of Vocational Psychology, Theory, Research and Practice*. London: LEA.

Super, D.E. and Bachrach, P.B. (1957) *Scientific Careers and Vocational Development Theory*. New York: Teachers College Press.

Swanson, J.L. (1996) The theory is the practice: Trait-and-factor/person-environment fit counseling, in M.L. Savickas and B.W. Walsh (eds) *Handbook of Career Counseling Theory and Practice*. Palo Alto, CA: Davis-Black Publishing.

Thorndike, R.L. and Hagen, E. (1959) *Ten Thousand Careers*. New York: John Wiley & Sons.

Tyler, L.E. (1961) *The Work of the Counselor*, 2nd edn. New York: Appleton.

Van Esbroeck, R. and Watts, A.G. (1997) Training for new skills for a holistic guidance model. Paper presented at the VIth FEDORA Conference, L'Aquila, Italy.

Walsh, A. (1999) *Individual Learning News*. Sudbury: DfEE.

Walsh, B.W. (1990) A summary and integration of career counseling approaches, in W.B. Walsh and S.H. Osipow (eds) *Career Counseling: Contemporary Topics in Vocational Psychology*. London: LEA.

Walsh, B.W. and Osipow, S.H. (eds) (1983) *Handbook of Vocational Psychology, Vol. 2, Applications*. London: LEA.

Walsh, B.W. and Osipow, S.H. (1990) *Career Counseling: Contemporary Topics in Vocational Psychology*. London: LEA.

Watkins, C.E. and Savickas, M.L. (1990) Psychodynamic career counseling, in W.B. Walsh and S.H. Osipow (eds) *Career Counseling*. London: LEA.

Watt, G. (1996) *The Role of Adult Guidance and Employment Counselling in a Changing Labour Market – Final Report on EUROCONSUL*, An Action Research Programme on Counselling and Long-Term Unemployment. Loughlinstown, Co. Dublin, Ireland. Stourbridge: ICG.

Watts, A.G. (1996) Careers work in higher education, in A.G. Watts, B. Law, J. Killeen, J.M. Kidd and R. Hawthorn (eds) *Rethinking Careers Education and Guidance*. London: Routledge.

Watts, A.G. (1999) Mind over a matter of exclusion. Social and moral dilemmas lie at the heart of social exclusion. *Career Guidance Today*, 7 (1): 18–26.

Watts, A.G. and Esbroeck, R. (1998) *New Skills for New Futures: Higher Education Guidance and Counselling Services in the European Union*. Brussels: VUB Press.

Watts, A.G. and McCarthy, J. (1998) *Community-Based Guidance and Social Exclusion*, Briefing Paper. NCGE/NICEC.

Watts, A.G., Law, B., Killeen, J., Kidd, J.M. and Hawthorn, R. (eds) (1996) *Rethinking Careers Education and Guidance*. London: Routledge.

Wijers, G.A. and Meijers, F. (1996) Careers guidance in the knowledge society. *British Journal of Guidance and Counselling*, 24 (1): 185–98.

Williams, L. (1996) *The Careers Service and Consumer Councils. A Development Project for Cornwall and Devon Careers Limited*. Choice and Careers Division/QADU. Sudbury: DfEE.

Williamson, E.G. (1939) *How to Counsel Students: A Manual of Techniques for Clinical Counselors*. New York: McGraw-Hill.

Williamson, E.G. (1949) *Counseling Adolescents*. New York: McGraw-Hill.

World Health Organization (1992) *The ICD-10 Classification of Mental and Behavioral Disorders*. Geneva: WHO.

Winnicott, D.W., Winnicott, C., Shepherd, R. and Davis, M. (eds) (1988) *Babies and Their Mothers*. London: Free Association Books.

Wrenn, C.G. (1958) Editorial. *Journal of Counseling Psychology*, 5: 242.

Wrenn, C.G. (1964) Human values and work in American life, in H. Borow (ed.) *Man in a World at Work*. Boston, MA: Houghton Mifflin.

Young, R. and Collin, A. (eds) (1992) *Interpreting Career Hermeneutical Studies of Lives in Context*. Westport, CT: Praeger.

Index

COUNSELLING FOR YOUNG PEOPLE

Judith Mabey and Bernice Sorensen

This book gives a wide picture of the diversity of counselling services available to young people in Britain today, with special focus on schools and young people's counselling services. It sets these services in their historical context and describes how they have evolved. The book puts forward theoretical models for working with young clients and discusses counselling issues as they relate to work with this age group. In addition it considers some of the pitfalls counsellors may encounter in working alongside other professionals and within agencies. It includes discussion on ethical issues, non-discriminatory practice, confidentiality and child protection. The book is enlivened by case material and by examples of good practice and interesting initiatives from around the country. It will be of particular interest to counsellors, teachers, youth workers, social workers and counselling students interested in working with this age group.

Features
- Illustrated throughout with case material
- Wide discussion of ethical issues
- Examples of good practice and new initiatives
- Gives theoretical models for counselling young people

Contents
The development of counselling for young people – Counselling for young people – The practice of counselling for young people – Specific issues in counselling for young people – Professional relationships in counselling for young people – A critique of counselling for young people – Appendix – References – Index.

160pp   0 335 19298 X (paperback)

COUNSELLING AND SOCIAL WORK

Judith Brearley

Social work is perennially in the public eye, and interest in counselling
has never been greater. But these activities are changing rapidly in
response to new needs and resource limitations, and their complexity is
not easy to grasp even by those involved. This book looks at how the
specific context of social work shapes the nature of counselling in terms
of both opportunities and constraints. How can social workers integrate
the counselling dimension of the job with other roles expected of them?
What training, supervision and support do they need? How do they
collaborate with other professions? Above all, how do they effectively
deal with people's private troubles, subjective feelings and disrupted
relationships (the traditional concern of counselling), whilst simultaneously fulfilling statutory requirements and involving themselves
in the contentious politics of social provision? A disturbing situation
is revealed, in which such role conflicts, coupled with media pressure
and policy changes, are undermining the professional competence and
confidence of social workers, thus depriving the most needy people of
help. A fresh understanding of insights from counselling is seen as
providing a partial answer to this serious state of affairs.

Contents

*The development of counselling in social work – The context of counselling in
social work – The practice of counselling in social work – Specific issues in
counselling in social work – Professional relationships in counselling in social
work – A critique of counselling in social work – References – Index.*

160pp   0 335 19002 2 (paperback)